ECHOES OF WAR DRUMS

The Civil War in Mountain Maryland

by
James Rada, Jr.

LEGACY
PUBLISHING

A division of AIM Publishing Group

ECHOES OF WAR DRUMS:
THE CIVIL WAR IN MOUNTAIN MARYLAND

Published by Legacy Publishing, a division of AIM Publishing Group.
Gettysburg, Pennsylvania.
Copyright © 2013 by James Rada, Jr.
All rights reserved.
Printed in the United States of America.
First printing: November 2013.

Portions of this book first appeared in the *Cumberland Times-News*, *Maryland Life Magazine*, *Wonderful West Virginia Magazine* and *Allegany Magazine*.

ISBN 9780971459991

LEGACY
PUBLISHING

315 Oak Lane • Gettysburg, Pennsylvania 17325

CONTENTS

War Comes to Allegany County 5
Cumberland's Importance to the War Effort... 8
Cumberland Gets Help From the Battlefield Angels 12
The Military Occupies Cumberland 21
Civil War Tensions Led to Cumberland Riot 25
Garrett County's Civil War Forts... 30
The Hero of Philippi Comes to Cumberland..................................... 32
The Confederate Army Attack at New Creek 37
Allegany Countians Protecting Allegany County 40
The Mount Savage Iron Works Warrior 43
Who Wins When Both Sides Retreat? 47
Boating the Border of Warring Nations 50
Consolidating Civil War Hospitals at Clarysville 57
The Monitor, The Merrimack and Cumberland 61
A Reporter's View of Cumberland During the War 72
The Battle of Antietam 75
A Confederate Post Office in Cumberland 78
Clarysville Hospital Doctor Faces Court Martial 81
The Day Cumberland was in the Confederacy................................. 84
The Banishment of a Confederate Family.. 91
C&O Canal President Imprisoned for Treason 94
John Garrett Used the Railroad to Help the Union 97
Cumberland's Biggest Civil War Battle... 100
Oldtown's Civil War Skirmish... 104
Military Justice in Cumberland 107
Teenage Rebellion, Civil War Style... 110
A Pair of Generals Gives Confederates an Ace in the Hole........... 113
In the Wake of Assassination... 124
Both Armies Wanted Romney, Neither One Could Hold It........... 126
Reburying the Dead... 130
Honoring Those Who Served in the Civil War 136
How Antietam was Remembered 50 Years Later 139
Who is "Genl. Scofield"? 143
Maryland's Last Confederate Son.. 146

CRITICAL ACCLAIM FOR THE WORKS OF JAMES RADA, JR.

Saving Shallmar

"But Saving Shallmar's Christmas story is a tale of compassion and charity, and the will to help fellow human beings not only survive, but also be ready to spring into action when a new opportunity presents itself. Bittersweet yet heartwarming, Saving Shallmar is a wonderful Christmas season story for readers of all ages and backgrounds, highly recommended."

- *Small Press Bookwatch*

Battlefield Angels

"Rada describes women religious who selflessly performed life-saving work in often miserable conditions and thereby gained the admiration and respect of countless contemporaries. In so doing, Rada offers an appealing narrative and an entry point into the wealth of sources kept by the sisters."

- *Catholic News Service*

Canawlers

"A powerful, thoughtful and fascinating historical novel, Canawlers documents author James Rada, Jr. as a writer of considerable and deftly expressed storytelling talent."

- *Midwest Book Review*

Between Rail and River

"The book is an enjoyable, clean family read, with characters young and old for a broad-based appeal to both teens and adults. Between Rail and River also provides a unique, regional appeal, as it teaches about a particular group of people, ordinary working 'canawlers' in a story that goes beyond the usual coverage of life during the Civil War."

  - *Historical Fiction Review*

Canawlers

"James Rada, of Cumberland, has written a historical novel for high-schoolers and adults, which relates the adventures, hardships and ultimate tragedy of a family of boaters on the C&O Canal. ... The tale moves quickly and should hold the attention of readers looking for an imaginative adventure set on the canal at a critical time in history."

  - *Along the Towpath*

OTHER BOOKS BY JAMES RADA, JR.

Fiction

Beast (e-book)

Between Rail and River

Canawlers

Kachina (e-book)

Kuskurza (e-book)

Logan's Fire

My Little Angel (e-book)

October Mourning

The Race (e-book)

The Rain Man

Non-Fiction

Battlefield Angels: The Daughters of Charity Work as Civil War Nurses

Beyond the Battlefield: Stories from Gettysburg's Rich History (e-book)

Kidnapping the Generals: The South's Most-Daring Raid Against the Union (e-book)

Looking Back: True Stories of Mountain Maryland

Looking Back II: More True Stories of Mountain Maryland

A Love Returned (e-book)

No North, No South…: The Grand Reunion at the 50th Anniversary of the Battle of Gettysburg

Saving Shallmar: Christmas Spirit in a Coal Town

When the Babe Came to Town: Stories of George Herman Ruth's Small-Town Baseball Games (e-book)

For Ben who dreams of being a soldier.

1

War Comes to Allegany County

When Abraham Lincoln was elected the 16th President of the United States in 1860, Allegany County saw little reason to celebrate. In the four-person race, Lincoln had finished dead last, according to William Lowdermilk in *A History of Cumberland, Maryland*.

Lincoln's candidacy had also not been endorsed by any of the local newspapers. John Bell of the Constitutional Union Party, endorsed by the *Civilian and Telegraph*, carried the county with 1,521 votes. Stephen Douglas, seen as Lincoln's main competition, received 1,202 votes and the endorsement of the *Democratic Alleganian*. John Breckinridge, endorsed by the *Bulletin*, received 980 votes. Lincoln received only 522 votes.

Bell would go on to win three states in the election Virginia, Kentucky and Tennessee, but Lincoln became president.

Lincoln's election led to South Carolina's secession and started the debate over how many other states would follow. Maryland was one of those states where debate was heated. The election of 1860 had barely finished before campaigners for and against secession began appearing.

Public meetings, demonstrations and parades happened all around Allegany County as both sides sought supporters. However, just as the election results showed Allegany County had diverse opinions on leadership of the country, the secession debate showed that issue also wasn't so cut and dried for county residents.

The Friends of the Union was a group against secession while at the same time saying it agreed that the North was hostile towards the South. Another group that sought support was the Conditional Unionists who wanted Maryland to remain neutral if war broke out.

"Public discussion now affected private relationships. Old friends became alienated, visits and receptions were canceled, and the sermons and prayers of ministers were scrutinized for evidence of political sympathies," David Dean wrote in *Allegany County – A History.*

John Bell and his running mate, Edward Everett, carried Allegany County in the 1860 Presidential election. Photo courtesy of Wikimedia Commons.

Once the fighting began in April 1861 and the president issued a call for troops, much of the debate had to end as men made their choices and that choice was to support the Union. "Two days after Lincoln's first call for troops, Lonaconing had formed its own company, begun regular drills, and telegraphed the Secretary of War in Washington for marching orders," Dean wrote.

According to Dean, the county would have the greatest success among all Maryland counties in not only meeting its enlistment quota but exceeding. For instance, during the October 1862 draft, Allegany County was required to enlist 872 men either as volunteers or draftees. The final count showed that 1,463 men joined.

Not all of Allegany County's fighting men made for the nearest Union company, though. Those men who were strong in their Southern sympathies, crossed the Potomac River and joined a company in Virginia.

As a symbol of Cumberland's Union support, a large American flag was draped between the St. Nicholas Hotel and Belvidere Hall by an unknown group of Union supporters. Many thought the patriotic display would cause problems with those residents who had Southern sympathies, but nothing happened at that time.

However, on May 29, 1861, in what would become a popular target for Southern sympathizers, the Baltimore and Ohio Railroad bridge over Patterson Creek and the Chesapeake and Ohio Canal was burned. It was attempt to stop or at least slow one of the Union's main transportation arteries.

War had come to Allegany County.

2
Cumberland's Importance to the War Effort

Though no historic battles were fought in Cumberland during the Civil War, the city and Allegany County were strategic to the Union victory.

Why?

Three reasons. The Baltimore and Ohio Railroad. The Chesapeake and Ohio Canal. The National Road. They all ran through the city.

If Cumberland had fallen to the Confederate Army for an extended time, then supply lines and troop transport could have been disrupted. The B&O Railroad could easily move supplies and troops from Washington to Baltimore to points west. The C&O Canal brought needed coal into Washington and provided limited troop transport. The National Road provided a maintained route that made it easier to move wagons and heavy artillery across the mountains.

The B&O Railroad was an early target of Confederate troops because portions of the railroad's route passed into Virginia (and after 1863, West Virginia). This made it convenient for Confederate troops to capture trains and tear up tracks. About a month after the war began, B&O Railroad bridges at Patterson's Creek and over the C&O Canal at North Branch were destroyed. Such guerilla tactics would continue through much of the war.

In order to try and better protect the railroad and its assets, a special military district was created whose boundaries matched those of the railroad, but its length stretched military forces charged with protecting it thin.

"Protecting the railroad was a herculean task," Harold Scott wrote in *The Civil War Era in Cumberland, Maryland and nearby Keyser, West Virginia (1861-1865)*.

"The means of defense consisted largely of placing detachments of men at important , and at all tunnels. Pickets patrolled other parts of the line. Garrisons at Cumberland, and nearby Hancock, New Creek, and Romney, from time to time provided troops for some of this duty."

Cumberland's Baltimore Street as it appeared during the Civil War. Photo courtesy of the Library of Congress.

Later in the war, innovations like blockhouses and armored railroad cars were introduced with some success in helping the Union with the defenses.

The C&O Canal faced even more problems than the railroad. Not only did the Canal Company have to deal with Confederate Army damage, but its own suppliers and Mother Nature helped shut it down at times. Early in the war, coal miners in Allegany County and canal boatmen both went on strike for higher wages. Even after this was settled, the canal company still had problems keeping the canal open.

Confederate forces had attempted to destroy the stone aqueducts that carry the canal across rivers and culverts but had quickly found that the construction work was so well done that it would take too long to be successful. Instead they concentrated mainly on burning lock doors or damaging the berm.

Following the Battle of Folck's Mill near Cumberland in August 1864, Confederate forces retreated down Oldtown Road in the hopes of crossing into West Virginia over Cresap's Bridge. However, the 153rd Ohio Infantry destroyed the bridge and took up a position on Alum Hill in an attempt to trap the Confederate forces in Maryland until Union reinforcements could arrive.

Confederate artillery pounded the hill, but the Union troops held their position and were able to keep the Confederate soldiers from escaping. One battalion tried to cross at an unguarded section of the river but couldn't. Confederates even tried to use the wreckage of the bridge to create a new crossing and that, too, was unsuccessful. Armor train cars from Cumberland arrived to turn the tide and force the Confederates to find another way home.

While the Union had prevailed, the fighting had left the canal so damaged that the Washington Star noted that the time needed to repair the damage would "keep back over a hundred thousand tons of coal from the Washington market this season."

The attacks and shut downs may have been a hindrance to the Union war effort, but they were devastating to the local economy in Cumberland.

"Her great thoroughfare, the Baltimore and Ohio Railroad, was interrupted and her Canal closed. Trade from Virginia was withdrawn. Every industry was stopped or curtailed; stores were closed and marked 'for rent;' real estate sank rapidly in value. Merchants without customers slept at their counters, or sat at the doors of their places of business. Tradesmen and laborers, out of employment, lounged idly about the streets. The railroad workshops were silent and operations in the mining regions almost entirely ceased. Then commenced a deep, painful feeling of insecurity and an undefined dread of the horrors of war. Panic makers multiplied and infested society, startling rumors were constantly floating about of secret plots and dark conspiracies against the peace of the community and private invidivuals," William Lowdermilk wrote in *A History of Cumberland, Maryland.*

3

Cumberland Gets Help From the Battlefield Angels

It's uncertain who pleaded with the Sisters of Charity of Cincinnati to care for the thousands of wounded soldiers who filled the hotels, churches and warehouses of Cumberland during the Civil War. Three people are credited with making the case for the sisters' help in the city. What is certain is that the sisters responded quickly to the call for help.

"On the 16th of February 1861 – there came a hasty call for Sisters of Charity to go to Cumberland, Md. to nurse the sick and wounded soldiers. ...I had just a half hour to prepare for the journey," Sister Gabriella Crowe wrote after the war.

Though Cumberland was far from much of the fighting during the Civil War, the city sat along the Baltimore and Ohio Railroad line. This made it easy for wounded to be loaded onto trains near the battlefield and sent to Cumberland or other cities where more formal hospitals could be set up. Though the soldiers could receive better care at a hospital behind the lines, many of them were too injured or sick to survive the bumpy, crowded ride to the hospital. Those that did were much worse for wear when they arrived at Cumberland.

In less than a year, the city had quickly become a medical center where one out of four people were either sick or wounded.

Records show that the eight sisters, along with Mother Josephine Harvey and Father Edward Collins leave on the B&O Railroad on the afternoon of February 15th. In the rush to get to Cumberland, Dr. McMahon who was the sisters' escort on the trip missed the train. Sister Anthony O'Connell caught the train just in time and left on it thinking the other sisters had already boarded. They hadn't. They were still waiting for Dr. Mahon.

"Angels of the Battlefield" showing Sisters of Charity aiding wounded Civil War Soldiers. Courtesy of the Sisters of Charity of Cincinnati.

Sis. Anthony got as far as Columbus, Ohio, when she received a telegram from Archbishop John Purcell that read, "Return at once. Two boat loads of wounded soldiers from Pittsburg Landing, to be cared for!" Most likely, these were wounded from the fighting at Fort Donelson, which was going on in Tennessee at the time, which is where Pittsburg Landing was located.

With Sis. Anthony no longer part of the group, the remaining sisters, Dr. McMahon and Rev. Collins finally left for Cumberland around 8 p.m. They reached Wheeling, Va., (West Virginia would not become a state until the following year) at noon the next day. They stayed the night at the Visitation Convent there. They left the following morning on February 17 "in a blinding snowstorm" and reached Cumberland in the evening.

Dr. George Suckley, the medical director in Cumberland, met the sisters at the train station and walked them down the street to a hotel that had been confiscated by Union army. Their appearance on the street drew a crowd of gawkers to whom Catholic sisters were an unfamiliar sight. At the hotel, the sisters took supper in the dining room.

"While we were waiting for supper the windows were besieged without by children, white and black, peeping in to see the curiosity," wrote Sis. Gabriella Crowe.

Sis. Sophia Gilmeyer

With the shortage of rooms in the city, the Sisters of Charity slept their first night in Cumberland on the floor in a reception room of the hotel that was filled with soldiers.

Dr. McMahon took them on a tour of the hospital facilities in Cumberland the next day. Large buildings including some of the warehouses along the Chesapeake and Ohio Canal had been confiscated for use as hospitals.

Sis. Mary Agnes Phillips

The hospitals had been set up so that the first floor was used for general purposes, such as housekeeping, cooking, storage, etc. while the upper floors had wards for the sick. On average, the hospitals held about 50 beds each, though they were often overcrowded after major battles. At the time, Cumberland had 14 hospitals overcrowded with more than 2,200 sick soldiers.

Most of the patients at this time were suffering from typhoid, pneumonia or erysipelas. According to *Baltimore Catholic Messenger*, the men were from Gen. Frederick Lander's division who had suffered from exposure while camped on the banks of Potomac and Patterson's Creek during the cold winter. Lander would die from his illness in March.

As the Sisters of Charity began to assume nursing duties in Cumberland, they quickly learned that the hospitals weren't that well supplied. They began making lists of what they would need to remedy that situation. The other problem they found was harder to deal with.

"The accommodations were poor, the weather cold, and the hospitals of which they were twelve, at some distance from one another, making it difficult, impossible for seven Sisters to give proper attention to the poor sufferers," Sis. Ambrosia Schwartz wrote.

After visiting each hospital building, the Sisters of Charity retired to find that a more-proper room had been found for them. Father Collins took them to the home of a Dr. Healy who was a Southern sympathizer. The doctor had fled Cumberland with the arrival of the Union army and had been commissioned a captain in the Confederate army. His wife, however, had remained behind.

Because of her husband's sympathies, the army had felt free to confiscate nearly all of the items in the house, leaving the woman so destitute that she needed to take in boarders to survive.

"This lady manifested much kindness towards us, but this went no further than words as all her property had been confiscated, she was often obliged to accept our provisions to sustain life," Sis. Agnes Phillips wrote.

The sisters now had rooms, but their beds not much better than the floor of the hotel. The beds were rough boards covered with straw ticks and pillows stuffed with straw.

The sisters then settled in for what would be a three-month stay in Cumberland. The work would be challenging and never finished.

Sis. Gabriella Crowe

When the thousands of wounded and sick soldiers in Cumberland threatened to overload the city's ability to care for them, they called for help from the Sisters of Charity of Cincinnati. The sisters were one of the few groups in the country at the time that had any professional nursing experience and they were more than willing to help.

"We are delighted also at the arrival of the Sisters, chiefly at this time, when so many once robust and stout men, young and old, are now lying prostrate in hospitals in the midst of strangers, far from their home, dear friends and relations, but whose hearts will soon my gladdened and whose sad condition will soon be ameliorated by the constant, tender, and more than maternal care of the Sisters of Charity," one official wrote the Quartermaster General.

Sis. Ambrosia Schwartz

Seven Sisters of Charity came to Cumberland in February 1862 to help care for the 2,200 sick and wounded soldiers in makeshift hospitals throughout the town. Besides working as nurses, the sisters also took on the duties of cooks, housekeepers and hospital administrators.

"The sick men seem astonished and cannot comprehend the devotedness, the zeal and unwearying patience of the Sisters. Some declared that had the Sisters been here from the beginning, not a man would have died," the *Baltimore Mirror* reported.

Sis. Ambrosia Schwartz wrote that their duties were fatiguing and often disgusting because of the blood and wounds they had to deal with. However, due to the hard work and management of other workers by the Sisters of Charity, the hospitals soon became cleaner and the food better suited to something for wounded men to eat.

"One poor fellow said to me, Oh! Mother had you and your Sisters come sooner many of our poor boys would not be dead. He said no one could have any idea what they have suffered and endured for want of care and proper nursing. One poor fellow they say, a few hours before he died wrote on the wall by his bed that his lips had not been wet for the last 24 hours. Others they say were found dead in their beds & from appearances had been dead sometime. They have been dying very fast for the last few weeks but at present the number is decreasing. Only 7 have been reported in the dead house today. This is the lowest number they have had for the last six weeks. We have only lost one and he was in a dying condition when we took charge. All the other poor fellows are doing well. They know not how to express their gratitude to the Sisters for their kind attention to them," Sis. Sophia Gilmeyer wrote.

Not everyone was thrilled to see the sisters arrive in Cumberland. They met with some resistance early on because of the anti-Catholic bias in the country at the start of the war, but their devotion to the patients soon won them over.

Sis. Jane Garvin was working in a ward late one night when an ambulance arrived with wounded soldiers. One young soldier had a bad shoulder wound that the surgeon dressed and asked Sis. Jane to watch him through the night. Whenever Sis. Jane approached the soldier, he closed his eyes and pretended to be asleep. The next morning the surgeon redressed the wound with Sis. Jane assisting.

Sis. Jane Garvin

"I assisted all through, but not a word from his lips. He avoided my every look. I plainly perceived he had no love for the Catholic Church or her children," Sis. Jane wrote.

Sis. Mary Garvin

The soldier watched her as she went about her work. He never said a word to her, though. Finally, after a few days, he said to her, "Sister, I would like to be baptized. I have been a very, very bad man." It was a request with which she gladly complied.

The sisters own spiritual needs were taken care of by Father Collins and Redemptorist Fathers who had a monastery on the opposite side of the Potomac River. In order to assist with morning Mass, the sisters had to get up before daybreak to walk to cross the river in order to reach the monastery.

"We were frequently called upon to give the countersign the sentinel being unable to distinguish who we were in the early dawn, and once when the sentinels crossed bayonets upon our breasts the bravest of us trembled," Sis. Ambrosia wrote.

Despite their success at caring for the men and converting others, the Sisters of Charity also experienced the death of the soldiers for whom they cared.

"Many I think died of broken hearts. Faces and voices haunt me yet, calling for home and dear ones whom they were destined never to behold on earth," Sis. Agnes Phillips wrote.

Such was the state of medical care in those days that it would be another century before battle wounds took more lives than infection and disease during a war.

The sisters weren't left untouched by the death around them either. Years later, Sis. Ambrosia would recall, "Sad and numerous were the scenes we witnessed in these hospitals, and yet this morning none presents itself more vividly in my mind, than the boy-child I might say, who begged so hard for a gooseberry pie. Over and over he did accost me—'Where is my gooseberry pie?' Such a pie, I presume as his own dear distant mother had often made for him. Oh! how those poor fellows missed their mothers, and murmured their names sleeping and waking."

After three months some of the sisters returned to Cincinnati to care for wounded soldiers who were coming into the city from Richmond and Nashville. Other sisters were sent to New Creek to care for the wounded there.

4

The Military Occupies Cumberland

If it hadn't been for the rifles, you might have thought a circus had come to Cumberland in June 1861 as hundreds of men marched out of the morning fog and down Baltimore Street dressed in red-visor French caps, blue and red Greek jackets, gray twill breeches and buttoned gaiters, according to Lew Wallace in his autobiography. Other men were mounted on fine-looking horses.

It wasn't a circus parade, though. The country was at war and the men were the 11th Indiana Zouaves, commanded by Col. Wallace. The unit was patterned after a French Algerian unit that was known for its fighting skills, tactics and discipline.

After making their presence known in town on June 10, the infantry set up their camp on Rose Rill where Allegany High currently sits, according to William Lowdermilk in *A History of Cumberland, Maryland*.

"Many other Civil War units would be stationed in Cumberland as the war progressed, including the Second Regiment, Potomac Home Brigade, consisting of Allegany County recruits, but Wallace and his Zouaves would be the first to graphically dispel any illusions that some of the citizens of Allegany County may have had that the trauma of a Civil War might somehow pass them by," David Dean wrote in *Allegany County – A History*.

The federal government believed Allegany County to be strongly Union so the troops weren't in town so much to quell any Confederate sympathizers, but to protect the town's strategic position and resources. Cumberland was the endpoint of the Chesapeake and Ohio Canal, a major stop on the Baltimore and Ohio Railroad and the beginning of the National Road. The region also supplied much of the coal to Washington.

Gen. Robert Patterson commanded the military department of Pennsylvania, which included Allegany County at this point in the war. Patterson wrote a dispatch from his headquarters in Chambersburg, PA, noting Wallace's arrival in Cumberland. In his orders to Wallace, he wrote that the colonel should "Gather as much reliable information as possible of the disposition of the people of Maryland and Virginia in that vicinity." He also gave Wallace permission to use spies to gather his information.

Sgt. Francis E. Brown was a New York Zouave during the Civil War. Courtesy of Wikimedia Commons.

Soon after their arrival, Wallace learned that Confederate forces were occupying Romney and raiding the railroad at will from there. Wallace took 500 men on the railroad to Piedmont. From there, they marched overnight to Romney where they cleared out the Confederate forces with a minimum of trouble.

Patterson also recognized that the appearance of Union troops in Cumberland might upset the residents. He told Wallace, "By a kind, yet firm, course on your part, and by the good deportment of your troops, secure the confidence and good-will of the community in which you may be located. Let the inhabitants feel you are in their midst as friends and protectors."

Wallace reported that he was well received in Cumberland and he and his men tried to make the occupation as easy as possible. The Zouaves were encouraged to talk with the residents. The regimental band performed free concerts for the townspeople.

However, one glance at the newspapers and the notion of peaceful neighbors disappeared. "A 'hurrah for Jeff Davis' could bring the provost marshal from Cumberland to any area of the county, and common newspaper headlines were 'Arrested upon the Charge of Treason,' 'More Arrests,' or 'Another Arrest,'" Dean wrote.

Most of the Confederate sympathizers were taken to Cumberland where they were made to swear an oath of allegiance to the United States. However, high-profiles sympathizers were imprisoned. State Representative Josiah Gordon and State Senator Thomas McKaig were both imprisoned at locations outside of the county.

On June 19, word reached Wallace that 5,000 Confederate soldiers were marching on Cumberland from Romney. Residents didn't take the news well as "the entire population rushed into the streets, bells rang in every part of town, and the women and children were in a state of terror," James Thomas and T.J.C. Williams wrote in *A History of Allegany County*.

The Zouaves moved into action and took up defensive positions along Bedford Road just outside of Cumberland. In addition, about 100 men from Frostburg arrived to help with the defense within 20 minutes of the alarm sounding in Cumberland. Additional men from Grantsville, Centerville, Wellersburg and Bedford also arrived later.

What didn't arrive were the Confederate troops. It turned out to be a rumor gone wild.

Following some minor skirmishing outside of the city in the weeks to come, the Zouaves were order to join with Gen. Patterson's men in Martinsburg. They left Cumberland, but they would not be the last occupying military force in the city.

The Union encampment in Cumberland during the Civil War. From the Herman and Stacia Miller Collection courtesy of the Mayor and City Council of Cumberland, Md.

5

Civil War Tensions Led to Cumberland Riot

When the Civil War started, things grew tense in Cumberland, pro-Union and pro-Confederate residents argued over who was right or wrong, but for the most part, life continued as usual though more loudly.

"Even at social parties in parlors, ladies were transformed into violent politicians, and in their wild enthusiasm seemed ready to grasp the rifle and the sword and leave the nursery and the distaff to fainthearted, cowardly men and old women," William Lowdermilk wrote in *A History of Cumberland, Maryland.*

The May 1861 mayoral race in Cumberland saw the strong pro-Union candidate Col. C. M. Thurston defeat the incumbent mayor John Humbird, who was considered a pro-secession candidate. It had elevated the arguments between pro-Union and pro-secession parties to a new level. A large American flag was hung over Baltimore Street between the St. Nicholas Hotel and the Belvidere Hall. Although it was expected that this would cause some violence, it never happened.

"Mass meetings continued to be held almost nightly, but those of Southern sympathizers usually ended in confusion because of an inability to resolve the question of leaving the Union," David Dean wrote in *Allegany County – A History.*

Then in June of 1861, the Union Army arrived in Cumberland to ensure the Baltimore and Ohio Railroad remained open. Their protection was welcomed at first, but then citizens began realizing they had traded some of their freedom for that protection. In order to protect the city, the Union Army essentially placed Cumberland under martial law. Free speech was suppressed and any anti-Union talk was banned.

"Informers became busy. Citizens were arrested and marched under guard to the camp, and having received a lecture on loyalty and the crime of secession, were tendered the oath of allegiance and then permitted to return to their homes," Harold Scott wrote in *The Civil War Era in Cumberland, Maryland and nearby Keyser, West Virginia (1861-1865)*.

It was similar to the way that President Abraham Lincoln had treated Maryland in general in order to keep it in the Union. Confederate sympathizers were imprisoned in order to intimidate others and ensure that pro-Union officials remained in office.

Col. C. M. Thurston

While this heavy-handedness created calm on the surface, looks can be deceiving. Emotions that had been bled off bloodlessly previously through arguments now had no way to express themselves.

"Old friends became alienated and began to treat each other coolly. Visits were curtailed and often ended disagreeably. Associations and churches felt the disturbing influences. Ministers were interviewed, while their sermons and prayers were closely scrutinized for indications of political sentiments or sympathies," Lowdermilk wrote.

And so it built up until the point where it burst in a more violent way than any argument. The first signs of problems were when the bridges over Patterson's Creek and the Chesapeake and Ohio Canal were burned. However, this was easily turned to the advantage of the army as it became a reason to support that the Union Army needed to be in Cumberland to protect Western Maryland.

Then in late August, the problems hit closer to home.

Francis Thomas, a former governor and strong Unionist, had come out of retirement to run for and win a seat as a state representative. He returned to Western Maryland to help create support for forming the Potomac Home Brigade to help defend the Union and Western Maryland.

While speaking at a support rally to form the Potomac Home Brigade in downtown Cumberland, he was interrupted by a man who criticized the federal government. The crowd attacked the man, but he was defended by the editor of the *Democratic Alleganian*. When the crowd, which could now rightly be called a mob, finished with the heckler, "a large crowd of men at once made a descent on the office of 'The Alleganian,' which was Southern in its sympathies. The office was wholly destroyed, the material being thrown out of the window," Lowdermilk wrote.

The mob wasn't finished. The men left the destroyed office (the Alleganian would not resume publication until the end of the war) and went to the home of State Senator Thomas McKaig, where the YMCA is now. McKaig was a known secessionist, who along with three other Maryland officials met with Confederate President Jefferson Davis in May of 1861 "to convey the assurance that Maryland sympathized with the Confederate states, and that the people of Maryland were enlisted with their whole hearts on the side of reconciliation and peace," Thomas Scharf wrote in *History of Western Maryland*.

When the mob reached his house, they shouted and broke several of the windows, though no one was hurt.

This was only the start of the problems that Cumberland had under its quasi-martial law.

For much of the early part of the war, Gen. Benjamin Kelley was in command of the Union forces in the area. Though he cracked down on anti-Union talk in Cumberland, he generally only required the Confederate sympathizers to swear an oath of allegiance to the Union.

That changed in 1864 when Gen. David Hunter took command of the Department of West Virginia, which included Allegany County. Hunter was much harsher in his treatment of sympathizers. During a campaign in the Shenandoah Valley, he had burned the homes and property of anyone who aided the Confederate troops and thus, opposed him.

The Alleganian.

CUMBERLAND, MARYLAND.

Tuesday Morning, May 24, 1864.

PUBLICATION OFFICE ON MECHANIC STREET, NEAR THE NATIONAL HOTEL.

Local News.

THE DRAFT FOR ALLEGANY COUNTY.

Official List of those Drawn.

TOTAL NUMBER DRAFTED 87.

The following is the official list of persons drafted into the service of the United States from this county, which has been furnished us by the County Provost Marshal, Daniel Duncan, Esq. There were 14 drawn from the Market House District, and none from the Court House District, its quota having been raised by volunteers:

Cumberland — Market House District.

Thomas W. Shryer,	Frederick Beck,
Samuel Geary,	Joseph Bakeler,
Andrew Kammer,	Jacob Gross,
Henry Capp,	George Dryer,
August Zimmerman,	James W. Donnelly,
William Rawlings,	Joseph J. Wegman,
Rev. George Fosseler.	William McGittigan.

A clipping from the *Alleganian* newspaper, which a mob destroyed at the beginning of the Civil War. Courtesy of *Whlibr.org*.

Henrietta Lee in Jefferson County, West Virginia, was one of the people who had her home burned because of Hunter. She wrote to him in Cumberland, saying, "Oh, earth, behold the monster! Can I say, 'God forgive you'? No prayer can be offered for you! Were it possible for human lips to raise your name heavenward, angels would thrust the foul thing back again, and the demons claim their own. The curses of thousands, the scorn of the manly and upright and the hatred of the true and honorable, will follow you and yours through all time, and brand upon your name infamy! INFAMY!"

In Cumberland, the homes of Sprigg S. Lynn and Joseph Sprigg were burned because of their Southern sympathies. The McKaig family was exiled from Cumberland because Sen. McKaig was a sympathizer.

Hunter was in the area only eight months until Kelley returned to command in February 1865. With Hunter gone and the war winding down, the tensions in the area began to return to point where friends could once again disagree without worry about being thrown into prison.

6

Garrett County's Civil War Forts

Western Maryland's Civil War forts made Fort Cumberland from more than 100 years earlier look like a palace. Fort Pendleton and Fort Alice were both located in Garrett County, though at the time it was still part of Allegany County.

The Confederate Army had started the construction of Fort Pendleton near Gorman in June 1861. It was named for Confederate Gen. William Pendleton who served as Gen. Robert E. Lee's chief of artillery. However, the Confederates abandoned the fort in July 1861 without a shot ever having been fired.

The 4th Ohio Infantry took over the unfinished fort in August and finished in by mid-September. "They cut timber between the hilltop fort and the river below; they dug trenches and built earthworks for nearly a mile down the hill and over its eastern slopes," according to Stephen Schlosnagle in his book, *Garrett County: A History of Maryland's Tableland*.

The Union Army used the fort to guard the approach to the old Northwest Turnpike bridge and stayed there until January of 1862.

The soldiers' service there was not distinguished. Schlosnagle wrote that Gen. Benjamin Kelley noted that "the troops of Fort Pendleton were prone to neglect picket duty, avoid blockading road, and preferred fishing to military service." The men also tore the wooden siding from a nearby church and used it for firewood.

Kelley told the commander, Capt. Joseph M. Goodwin that he would be dismissed from the military if he didn't control his men. Goodwin didn't, but Kelley never carried through on his threat, probably because everyone involved knew that the fort had no strategic value and it didn't really matter what the soldiers were doing. "Strategically, the structure was an almost total waste of time and money during the period that it was garrisoned," Schlosnagle wrote.

The second Garrett County fort had a purpose, but it was too small to effectively fulfill that purpose when it mattered.

Oakland resident and Civil War enthusiast John Rathger is working with the Garrett County Historical Society to develop a trail to the Fort Alice and put together a sesquicentennial event that includes the fort and the Confederate raid on Oakland. He said at the time of the 1863 raid on Oakland, Fort Alice was pretty much just rifle pits near the Baltimore and Ohio Railroad bridge over the Savage River. A blockhouse was added to the site later.

The test of the fort's defensive capability took place on April 26, 1863, when about 1,000 Confederate troops captured Oakland and the fort after firing only two shots.

"The first shot was from a sentry firing a warning shot for the people in Oakland, but nobody heard it because they were in church," Rathger said. "The second shot was fired at the sentry as the Confederate troops chased him. The shot took off his heel."

Confederate Gen. William Jones commanded the troops that included some of pll's Rangers and the 2nd Maryland Confederate Infantry unit.

"They had local men with them who knew the roads and territory who could help them through the area," Rathger said.

Oakland wasn't the Confederate target. They were heading toward Morgantown and Oakland was a target of opportunity. The Confederate troops arrested the Union soldiers stationed at the fort, burned the fort and the B&O bridge that the fort had been built to defend. The first group of Confederate troops came into Oakland at 11 a.m. and moved out by 3 p.m. Another group came through an hour later and passed through.

Though still in the planning stages, the Garrett County Historical Society and Oakland's Main Street Program will be sponsoring events to remember the capture of the town in April 2013.

7

The Hero of Philippi Comes to Cumberland

Protecting Allegany County and the surrounding area during the Civil War was just a job for Gen. Benjamin Kelley until he fell in love with Western Maryland and one young woman in particular.

Kelley was born in New Hampshire in 1807 and moved to Wheeling, Va., (it became West Virginia in 1863) as a young man looking to find his own way in the world. He worked there as a merchant until 1850 when he moved to Philadelphia, Pa., to take a job as a freight agent for the Baltimore and Ohio and Philadelphia and Washington railroads. That all changed in 1861 when the Civil War began.

While he had lived in Wheeling, Kelley had joined the Guards Military Company and later become commander of the 4th Virginia Volunteer Regiment. The regiment made up a large portion of the 1st Virginia Volunteer Regiment that formed at the start of the war.

"Although [Kelley] had been in Philadelphia for ten years, he resigned his position with the railroad, and returned to Wheeling to assume command of 'the first loyal regiment south of the Mason and Dixon's line,'" Harold Scott wrote in *The Civil War Era in Cumberland, Maryland and nearby Keyser, West Virginia (1861-1865)*.

The 1st Virginia Volunteers left Wheeling near the end of May 1861 and within a week, Kelley was leading them into a battle against Col. George Porterfield's men, although Kelley and his men were poorly equipped and had little ammunition. Kelley pressed his attack and Porterfield fell back from Grafton to Philippi. The Union army caught the Confederate army off guard (many were still sleeping in their tents) in the early morning hours of June 3. A few prisoners were taken and the Confederates were routed. However, during the fighting, Kelley was shot through the lung. It was believed that it would be fatal, but he managed to survive.

It took Kelley two months to recover. During his time in the hospital, not only did he receive numerous letters of praise for his actions, but he was promoted to brigadier general. When he returned to duty, he was given command of the railroad division in Grafton to protect the B&O Railroad and its assets from Cumberland to Grafton and Parkersburg.

General Benjamin Kelley

While executing his duties, he spent a lot of time in Cumberland since it was a major hub for the railroad. In October 1861, Kelley and his men captured Romney.

When Gen. Frederick Landers was wounded, Kelley was also given temporary command of the railroad division from Cumberland to Harpers Ferry. Landers resumed command in early 1862, but only for a short time until he got sick and eventually died. Kelley once again took command in April 1862 and he had his headquarters in Cumberland.

Kelley was given command of the Department of West Virginia

in June 1863. The department headquarters was in Clarksburg, W.Va., but Kelley moved it to Cumberland in November. He worked from there until March of 1864 when he was given a month leave of absence. During his leave, Gen. Franz Sigel took over Kelley's duties until he lost a battle with Confederate forces in New Market, Va. in May. Shortly thereafter, Gen. David Hunter took command of the Department of West Virginia.

Hunter had little tolerance for Southern sympathizers and he dealt with them harshly. During a campaign in the Shenandoah Valley in June 1864, he had burned the homes and property of anyone who aided the Confederate troops and thus, opposed him.

The relatively light hand of a military occupation under Kelley began to squeeze shut under Hunter's command. The homes of Sprigg S. Lynn and Joseph Sprigg were burned because of their Southern sympathies. In fact, Lynn was one McNeill's Rangers.

It would take Kelley to restore some sanity to the situation.

As Gen. David Hunter cracked down on Confederate sympathizers in Cumberland and Allegany County, the area began seeming more like an occupied Southern city rather than a Union city.

When Gen. Kelley returned to duty after a month's leave, it was hoped that he would resume his position in charge of the Department of West Virginia, which included Allegany County. Instead, he was given another former position he had held, which was the protection of the B&O Railroad and its property. This put Kelley in Cumberland from time to time, but he answered to Hunter when there.

As the commander of the area, Hunter ordered Kelley to burn the property of the McKaig family who were known Southern sympathizers. Kelley hadn't been around when the other properties of sympathizers had been burned nor had he been ordered to do the deed. This went too far for Kelley. He took the order back to Hunter and told the general that he would not obey it, according to the *Cumberland Daily Times* in 1891. Normally, disobeying an order would have a soldier arrested, but Kelley was a fellow general and a respected one so Hunter was more careful.

"Why do you ask this? Are not these people influential and dangerous enemies of the Union?" Hunter asked.

"They are undoubtedly Southern in their sympathies, but they had not committed any act that should subject them to such punishment.

The property owned by them is located in various parts of the city, and might result in a general conflagration that would destroy the city," Kelley responded.

It is not known which reason changed Hunter's mind, but from his past actions, it was probably the latter one. In any event, Hunter rescinded the order. Priscilla McKaig, her sister-in-law and their children were still banished from Cumberland and spent the next three months wandering through West Virginia.

"I would not go, they advised me to go—said perhaps they might use violence or force, we did not know what such a brute as Hunter might do," McKaig wrote in her journal.

Hunter's heavy-handed tactics with non-combatants led to Confederate "an eye for eye" retaliation. Confederate forces began burning northern towns. When Cumberland was targeted, Kelley and his men stopped the Confederate advance at the Battle of Folck's Mill. A grateful Cumberland threw a parade in his honor and the president promoted him to major general.

Kelley continued his defense of the B&O Railroad until February 1865. He was in Cumberland when McNeill's Rangers made a covert raid into town and kidnapped him and Gen. George Crook from their rooms and took them to Richmond where they were eventually ransomed.

The war ended shortly thereafter and Kelley resigned his commission near the end of May. He returned to Cumberland in May to marry Clare Bruce. It was his second marriage. His first wife had died in 1858.

Kelley worked at federal jobs for the next 22 years, retiring in 1887. Then he and his wife returned to live in Swan Meadows, which had been part of Allegany County during the war. However, Garrett County had formed from the western portion on Allegany County in 1876, which is where Kelley's retirement home was located.

"Most of his next four years was spent in a peaceful retirement," Harold Scott wrote in *The Civil War Era in Cumberland, Maryland and nearby Keyser, West Virginia (1861-1865)*.

Kelley died on July 16, 1891, and his funeral was held at St. Matthew's Protestant Episcopal Church in Oakland, but he was buried in Arlington National Cemetery, away from the land he loved.

Gen. Benjamin Kelley's grave marker. Courtesy of Wikimedia Commons.

8

The Confederate Army Attack at New Creek

Keyser, W.Va., was strategically located during the Civil War. From atop the hill where Potomac State College now sits, a relatively small force of soldiers could protect the Baltimore and Ohio Railroad and see an enemy force coming 50 miles away in some directions.

New Creek (Keyser's name during the Civil War) "was among the very first places occupied and fortified by Federal forces, General Lew Wallace taking possession early in June, 1861," Jack C. Sanders wrote in a "Brief History of Keyser, W.Va."

While the Union was quick to occupy the city, it wasn't always able to hold it. Confederate Rangers made quick raids against targets in the area. In fact, the first significant event for New Creek during the Civil War was when Confederates burned the bridge across the Potomac River near the city. By the end of the war, New Creek had changed hands between Union and Confederate forces 14 times. It was nowhere near the amount of times that Romney, W.Va., changed hands but it was enough to make New Creek residents uneasy.

To reinforce its position, the Union Army constructed Fort Fuller on the hill where Potomac State College sits and the smaller fortified positions of Fort Piano and Fort Williams further out so that they could act as an early warning system.

"Fort Fuller, situated on a hill and in sight of our camp, is rapidly going forward to completion. It will be exceedingly strong when finished and will command this entire valley. Troops are pouring in here daily in large numbers from Ohio and other places. Our canvass is rapidly spreading over more territory, each day looking more warlike than the preceding one," one soldier wrote to the newspaper, the *Reporter and Tribune* in December 1862.

The fort's walls were wooden and covered with sod. Platforms were constructed behind the walls where the batteries were placed. The fort had only one entrance, which made it easier to defend.

After the Battle of Folck's Mill in Cumberland in 1864, Confederate General John McCausland retreated with his men to Oldtown and then across the Potomac River to Springfield, W.Va. The army was allowed to rest there and McCausland also received reinforcements.

McCausland's men had burned Chambersburg, Pa., but then been thwarted from taking similar actions at Hancock and Cumberland. Now refreshed, McCausland still wanted to inflict some damage on the Union. He chose New Creek as his target.

Gen. John McCausland

McCausland and Confederate General Bradley Johnson set out New Creek on August 4, 1864. The city was considered lightly garrisoned with nine companies of the 154th Ohio Volunteer Infantry, two companies of the 6th West Virginia Volunteer Infantry; one company of the 2nd Maryland Volunteer Infantry, mounted; one section Battery L, 1st Illinois Light Artillery and one section Battery H, 1st West Virginia Light Artillery.

The Confederate Army began its attack around 1 p.m. on the outskirts of New Creek with a ferocity that drove the Union Army back into town towards Fort Fuller.

"There seemed to be no end to their numbers. They advanced in solid column until they reached a point about one mile from the fort, when they formed in line of battle stretching from the foot hills on our right to the mountain range on our left," according to Private Joseph Stipp, one of the soldiers with the 154th Ohio Volunteer Infantry.

Colonel Robert Stevenson, commander of the 154th, sent a dispatch to General Benjamin Kelley who was in command of the Union forces at Cumberland. It read: "We are attacked. The force is more than McNeill. They have infantry, cavalry, and artillery."

"McNeill" referred to McNeill's Rangers, a Confederate unit that made attacks in the region. The force was rarely more than 100 men. The small size allowed the company to attack quickly and then retreat.

Kelley sent a dispatch back that read, "Put your force in position and fight to the last. I will send the Eleventh to you."

The fighting continued and the Union held its ground. Around 4 p.m., four companies of the 11th West Virginia Volunteer Infantry arrived and joined the battle to the cheers and shouts of the defenders in and around Fort Fuller.

The fighting continued until darkness fell. Realizing that they did not have a large enough army to take the city, the Confederate Army left, heading towards Moorefield, W.Va. It was a welcome site that greeted the Union defenders in the morning.

"The very first dawn of the morning's gray light found us all on the alert waiting for some demonstration of the part of the enemy. Our feelings can better be imagined than described when we found the enemy had retired from our front and were nowhere to be seen. They had most gloriously repulsed and defeated, and were now seeking a more congenial clime." Stipp wrote.

9

Allegany Countians Protecting Allegany County

Francis Thomas was a former Speaker of the House for the Maryland legislature, five-term congressman who represented three different districts and former governor of Maryland. People had spoken of him as a Democratic Party nominee for the President of the United States. Though not from Allegany County (now Garrett County), it was here that he had chosen to retreat after his term had ended following his defeat for re-election. A nasty and public divorce led him to live the life of a recluse in the mountains until patriotism stirred his soul.

"Francis Thomas came down from his farm retreat on the Seventeen Mile Grade to rouse the citizenry of Allegany County," J. William Hunt wrote in the *Cumberland Sunday Times* in 1956.

First, Thomas sought and received authorization from the federal government to raise a military unit. In July 1861, Secretary of War Simon Cameron authorized Thomas to raise four regiments "for the protection of the Canal and of the property and persons of loyal citizens of the neighborhood and be stationed in the vicinity of the neighborhood," Thomas Scharf wrote in *History of Western Maryland*.

Thomas had the authorization printed on handbills and published in *The Civilian and Telegraph* newspaper. Then he began a campaign of public speeches in the area to rouse patriotic spirit and encourage men to enlist in the new brigade. He also met with local officials and civic groups to encourage them to support the formation of the military companies.

During one of Thomas's speeches in August, Confederate sympathizers heckled him. Upset at the disruption, "a large crowd of men at once made a descent on the office of 'The Alleganian,' which was

Southern in its sympathies. The office was wholly destroyed, the material being thrown out the window," William Lowdermilk wrote in *A History of Cumberland, Maryland.*

His energy and enthusiasm inspired hundreds of men to enlist as the Second Regiment Potomac Home Brigade, which was organized in the Allegany County from Aug. 21 to Oct. 31, 1861. Of the 10 companies in the brigade, nine were made up of Allegany County men, who signed up to serve three years.

"The military spirit ran high (especially) in Lonaconing and several important meetings were held and one in particular was notable," James Thomas and Judge T.J.C. Williams wrote in *History of Allegany County.* During that meeting, Dr. G. Ellis Porter, caught up in the spirit of the evening, climbed onto a table and gave a speech urging the men in attendance to help defend the Union cause. The men of Lonaconing responded and joined up in large numbers and Porter became a major in the Second Brigade.

The men of the Second Brigade initially fell under the command of General Benjamin Kelley who was charged with protecting the B&O Railroad and its property. Though the brigade didn't begin its official service as a unit until January 1862, as companies formed and were equipped, they were used as needed. Soldiers of the Second Brigade were engaged in skirmishes against Confederate forces as early as August 1861.

During much of their enlistment the soldiers of the Potomac Home Brigade lived according their name and served along the Potomac River from New Creek (Keyser) to east of Cumberland. They were involved in skirmishes in Springfield, W.Va.; Charlestown, W.Va.; Burlington, W.Va.; Moorfield Junction, W.Va. and Ridgeville, W.Va.

During one of their more-notable excursions, the Second Regiment was part of the army commanded by Gen. David Hunter in 1864 that burned Southern homes in the Shenandoah Valley southward until reaching Lynchburg, Va. The army also pursued the army of Confederate General Jubal Early into the South after the Battle of the Monocacy in 1864.

By the time the Civil War ended, 94 soldiers in the Second Brigade had been killed. This represented about 9 percent of the brigade's complement of men. Of those 94 men, one officer had been killed in action, nine enlisted men had been killed and action and the remainder died from disease or wounds, according to *History and Roster of the Maryland Volunteers*.

"That the Second (Regiment) Potomac Home Brigade fully sustained the reputation of Maryland soldiers for bravery and fidelity will never be questioned," Scharf wrote.

Allegany County also contributed significantly to the formation of the Third Regiment Potomac Home Brigade. This regiment started forming right after the Second Regiment filled up on Oct. 31, 1861, and continued recruiting until May 20, 1862. Of the 10 companies in this regiment, four were formed with men of Allegany County.

Francis Thomas

9

The Mount Savage Iron Works Warrior

He was the manager of the Mount Savage Iron Works who came from an upper middle class family in Massachusetts. His life should have been one of relative ease except that Charles Russell Lowell was a patriotic man.

"In his college class he was pre-eminent above all rivalry, yet, while marvelously apt in the direction of literature and philosophy, his stronger bent was towards the mechanic arts and practical life, and in this direction he easily and quickly attained high responsibilities and the breaking out of the war found him managing the Mount Savage Iron Works in Cumberland, Md., but on hearing of the attack in Baltimore upon the Massachusetts troops he dropped his work instantly and took the first train for that city," Charles A. Humphreys wrong in his book, *Field, Camp, Hospital and Prison in the Civil War 1863-1865.*

Lowell had been working at the Mount Savage Iron Works for less than a year when he resigned. The company had reopened in early 1860 after years of inactivity. It was later in the year that Lowell was brought on to manage the plant. The firing on Massachusetts soldiers by Baltimore civilians occurred in April 1861.

However, once he reached Baltimore, he discovered that both rail travel and telegraph communication with Washington had been cut off. He was then forced to walk to the city where he enlisted as an artilleryman.

By August 1861, Lowell had been commissioned a captain in the

6th U.S. Calvary. He served as Gen. George McClellan's aide-de-camp and fought next to the general in the 1862 Peninsula Campaign (service that saw him promoted to major) and 1862 Battle of Antietam.

"He was a born cavalier, high-spirited, quick, flashing his plans into instant orders to prompt execution; yet, with all this dashing, chivalrous spirit, he was always calm and self-possessed," Humphreys wrote.

Josephine Shaw and Charles Russell Lowell. Courtesy of Wikimedia Commons.

In one battle during the Peninsula Campaign in Slatersville, VA, a mounted Lowell was charging a Confederate soldier when the soldier aimed a double-barreled carbine at him.

"Drop that!" Lowell ordered.

So commanding was his voice, that the soldier actually started to lower his weapon before he came to his senses and fired at Lowell. He had lowered it enough, though, that the easy shot had missed Lowell.

During the Battle of Antietam, McClellan sent Lowell with orders for Gen. John Sedgwick. He found the men under heavy fire and on the verge of being routed. He set to work quickly rallying the men and galloping from point to point to give orders to the soldiers. He even had his horse shot out from under him, but he continued to rally the men.

"He seemed to fly from point to point, his eyes flashed fire, his voice shouted defiance, his sword pointed towards the foe, his horse caught his master's spirit, and they two, as one, put new courage into the flying troops, and so checked the rout which threatened disaster to the right of the Union line," Humphreys wrote.

In recognition of his bravery during the battle, McClellan allowed him to travel to Washington to present President Abraham Lincoln with the 39 standards captured in the battle.

During 1863, he organized the 2nd Massachusetts Cavalry and became its colonel. One of the highlights of this command was that his men were part of Battle of the Monocacy in the defense of Washington against Confederate Lt. Gen. Jubal Early. The Confederates reached the outskirts of the city but were repelled by smaller Union forces.

He continued to distinguish himself bravely until he was mortally wounded during the Union counterattack at the Battle of Cedar Creek on October 19, 1864. Gen. Philip Sheridan hurriedly tried to ensure that he was promoted to brigadier general on that day. Lowell died the following day in Middletown, Va. Despite Sheridan's efforts, Lowell wasn't nominated for brigadier general until two days after his death. Technically, he should not have received the promotion because he could not sign his commission, but Secretary of War Edwin Stanton made an exception for him.

When Lowell died, Sheridan said, "I do not think there is a quality I could have added to Lowell. He was the perfection of a man and a soldier. *I* could have been better spared."

He is buried in the Mount Auburn Cemetery in Cambridge, Mass.

11

Who Wins When Both Sides Retreat?

Sometimes you might really want something so badly that you're willing to work hard and sacrifice to get it. Then you get it, only to realize you really don't want it or need it. It's not just limited to the things you see on late-night infomercials. It can and has happened with ground fought for in the war.

Romney had an importance to Confederate troops in the war that was similar to Cumberland's importance to Union troops. Romney provided access to sabotaging both the Baltimore and Ohio Railroad and Chesapeake and Ohio Canal. Confederate troops also used the Northwest Turnpike, which ran along the current path of Route 50.

Gen. Benjamin Kelley was ordered to New Creek to gather his troops in October 1861. From there, there he was to gather his troops and go to Romney along the Northwest Turnpike and Mechanicsburg Gap and take the town.

"The order was swiftly executed, and early the morning of the 26th an expedition, consisting of twenty infantry companies, three pieces of artillery and the Ringgold Cavalry (22 Pennsylvania Cavalry) began the advance," Thomas Richards wrote in a 1963 article in *Tableland Trails*.

As part of the advance, Kelley ordered the second regiment of the Potomac Home Brigade to go through Frankfort and Springfield and enter Romney from the east. The Potomac Home Brigade was organized in Cumberland and made up of many men from Allegany County. Their objective was to cut off any Confederate retreat from the town and trap the troops in the town.

The Potomac Home Brigade commanded by Col. Thomas Johns met its first resistance within a mile of Springfield. Scouts from the

114th Virginia Militia fired on them, wounding two soldiers. The Brigade repelled the attackers and continued onward.

About 1 ½ miles south of Springfield, the road crossed the South Branch Potomac over a suspension bridge called "The Wire Bridge." It was built from wire cables with wooden flooring. Both the Union and Confederate forces realized the need to take and hold the bridge.

A Civil War battle re-enactment. From the Herman and Stacia Miller Collection courtesy of the Mayor and City Council of Cumberland, Md.

Lt. John Blue of the 114th Virginia Militia wrote, "To hold the bridge for any length of time, with the arms at hand (flintlocks, smooth bore muskets, shot guns, and home rifles), was an impossibility. The Colonel (Monroe) had placed his men in a position to hold, but a very bad one to let go . . . his men built a breastwork of stone on the upper (south) side of the bridge with a steep, rugged mountain immediately in the rear, up which his men would have to retreat at point blank range if driven from their position by a victorious enemy."

Shots were exchanged without anyone being wounded, but it was delaying the Brigade. Johns knew this could endanger Kelley's plan. Johns ordered Company A from Lonaconing and commanded by Capt. Alexander Shaw and Lt. John Douglas, to take the bridge. The company rushed the bridge only to find that the plank flooring had been removed. The Marylanders turned back only to have the Virginians fire on them as they retreated.

As Company A rejoined the rest of the Brigade, Johns made a decision. Before the attack on the bridge, he had heard shots in Romney and he assumed that Kelley had taken control of the town.

"Although Johns and his men had not taken Romney and cut off the Confederate retreat, the Colonel felt his mission accomplished as he had diverted some of the Virginia Militia from the main fight at the Mechanicsburg Gap. Therefore he ordered his command to retire northward to Oldtown, Maryland, where the force arrived at 9 p.m.," Richards wrote.

As the Marylanders retreated, the Virginians moved to cross the bridge. They were thwarted by Company B's troops who were covering the retreat of their fellow soldiers. However, the Virginians had heard the fighting in Romney, too. They reasoned that with the Union controlling the town, there was no need to hold the bridge so they retreated not only from Company B's shots but also from the area. They went east over the Jersey Mountain to regroup with other troops at the North River.

In the end, neither side held the bridge and both forces had retreated from the fight under fire.

12

Boating the Border of Warring Nations

While the Mason-Dixon Line being the dividing line between the North and the South, an argument could be made that the Chesapeake and Ohio Canal was the dividing line between the Union and Confederacy. Running alongside the Potomac River as it does, Virginia was directly south of the canal and Maryland was to the north. Whenever you read about an army crossing the Potomac River, it also had to cross the canal.

The unlucky location meant that the canal was vulnerable to destruction by both the Union and Confederate armies

"In some instances, battles were fought so close to the canal that the company's property was hurriedly made into hospitals and morgues," Elizabeth Kytle wrote in *Home on the Canal*.

The canal boats were considered military targets and Confederate soldiers made a habit of commandeering them at the start of the war and confiscating their cargo. One of these boats was owned by Cumberlander Thomas McKaig and held at Harpers Ferry until all the salt it was carrying in its holds was removed. Whether this was an act of piracy or not is debatable. Since McKaig was a Southern sympathizer, he might have made arrangements to deliver the salt to the Confederacy rather than the Union.

Early in the war, the Union Army seized the Alexandria Aqueduct and drained in to hinder any plans to canal boats and their cargo into Virginia and the primary cargo that everyone wanted was Allegany County coal.

"A specialized 'super-coal,' Maryland's product was particularly suited for New England textile mills and for steamship bunkering, and it had been used successfully for smelting iron. Thus, with Virginia coal no longer available to the northeastern market, Maryland's contribution became increasingly important to the Union Cause," National Park Service Historian Harlan Unrau wrote in *The Chesapeake and Ohio Canal During the Civil War: 1861-1865*.

Canal boat on the C&O Canal. The tow rope can be seen going out of the from on the right. Courtesy of the National Park Service.

Built to Last

The Confederate Army attempted multiple times to destroy the canal during the war or at least damage it so it wouldn't hold water, thereby stranding the canal boats and keeping the coal from reaching Washington.

Henry Kyd Douglas, a Marylander who served on Gen. Stonewall Jackson's staff wrote that the general made several trips to dam no. 5 in Washington County with the intent to destroy it "thereby impairing the efficiency of the Chesapeake and Ohio Canal, over which large supplies of coal and military stores were transported to Washington…"

However, Jackson and other Confederate officers soon found out that this wasn't as easy as it seemed. In December 1861, Jackson pounded the dam with artillery, but he couldn't breach it. Other officers had similar experiences when trying to destroy the canal. The masons who built the canal built it to last. Jackson's men finally resorted to digging a channel to divert water, causing the canal to dry up south of the dam. This left boats sitting in the canal and coal sitting in the warehouses in Cumberland that couldn't be shipped out.

Most of the damage to the canal was done early in 1861 and repaired before the First Battle of Bull Run except for a except Edwards Ferry, a culvert three miles above Paw Paw Tunnel, and the Oldtown Deep Cut. According to Unrau, "it took an 80-man crew with 20 horses and carts some 25 days to restore navigation at the large breach near the aforementioned culvert and the heavy rock slide at the Oldtown Deep Cut." While the last repairs were underway, General Robert Patterson dispatched a company of troops to Hancock to protect the waterway from Williamsport to Cumberland.

Canal boat on the C&O Canal. The tow rope can be seen going out of the from on the left. Courtesy of the National Park Service.

Problems in Cumberland

The disruption to the canal trade, along with the uncertainty of who controlled the B&O Railroad, sent Cumberland into an economic recession. William Lowdermilk wrote in *A History of Cumberland, Maryland,* "Her great thoroughfare, the Baltimore and Ohio Railroad, was interrupted and her Canal closed. Trade from Virginia was withdrawn. Every industry was stopped or curtailed; stores were closed and marked 'for rent;' real estate sank rapidly in value. Merchants without customers slept at their counters, or sat at the doors of their places of business. Tradesmen and laborers, out of employment, lounged idly about the streets. The railroad workshops were silent and operations in the mining regions almost entirely ceased. Then commenced a deep, painful feeling of insecurity and an undefined dread of the horrors of war. Panic makers multiplied and infested society, startling rumors were constantly floating about of secret plots and dark conspiracies against the peace of the community and private invidivuals,"

One of the lower locks of the C&O Canal near Washington, D.C. Courtesy of the National Park Service.

Protecting the Canal

Because of the problemns with raiders disrupting trade on the canal, President Abraham Lincoln had also authorized Representative Francis Thomas, a former president of the canal company in 1839-41, to organize four citizen regiments to protection canal property and boaters on the canal and along boat sides of the Potomac River. The companies would be called the Potomac Home Brigade.

While the lower sections of the canal saw heavy actions taken at times to destroy it, the upper sections saw relatively few problems. There were minor skirmishes and vandalism, but noting along the lines of what was seen on the canal below Williamsport.

It is believed that one of the reason that the upper sections of the canal weren't subject to the same attacks as the lower sections was that Canal President Alfred Spates had made an agreement with the Confederacy about military targets through an aide to General Robert E. Lee. While the agreement is known to have existed, the terms were never made public, according to Unrau.

A lock and lockhouse on the C&O Canal. Courtesy of the National Park Service.

Confiscation

The following spring, the ironclad *Merrimac* had officials in Washington fearing that their city could be bombarded. Desperate for a way to keep the dangerous, new sailing vessel out of the Potomac River, government officials commandeered more than 100 canal boats at Georgetown.

"Some were filled with rocks and taken down to the river so they could be sunk if it became necessary to block the channel. Six or eight of them actually were sunk later; the others were returned to their owners," Secretary of the Navy Gideon Welles wrote in his diary.

Boats were confiscated two other times during the year, but in the other instances not nearly as many boats were commandeered and they weren't kept from their work as long. When 40 boats were confiscated later in 1862, they were towed to another river to be used as bridges for Union troops to cross the river.

Cumberlander A.C. Greene, one of the canal directors, wrote to the Canal Company complaining that between the military actions against the canal and bad weather, "There has be no real navigation on the canal this year." He added that the "very existence of the canal" was "trembling in the balance." It would be impossible for the boatmen to replace in 1862 the 100 boats held by the government.

He wrote the letter in August and the following month, the Battle of Antietam occurred near the canal, shutting it down further. The tolls the Canal Company collected during September and August were less than 9 percent of the amount collected in 1860, which had been far from a banner year.

Oddly enough, as Union fortunes in the war began to turn following this battle so did the outlook for the canal. Business began to pick up the following year and would continue to grow throughout the war.

In Western Maryland, though, Confederate raiders shifted their focus from damaging the canal to destroying the boats. The raiders acted like pirates, capturing the boats, taking what they wanted and burning what was left.

"Rebs are stealing the horses from the Boats clear to Cumbd. Two boats have been robbed within ten miles of Cumbd. and last night a gang of McNeill's men crossed at Black Oak bottom, passed over Will's Mountain into the valley of Georges Creek and swept the coal mines of their horses. The American Co. lost sixteen," Greene wrote to the Canal Company.

When to war ended, the C&O Canal "emerged from the Civil War on both a depressing note and a promising one." The canal had been abused during the war and left in deplorable condition so much so that it wouldn't be until 1869 that all of the damage done from the Civil War was repaired. However, trade on the canal had started rising in 1863 and would continue to grow and remain strong through the canal's golden years of the 1870s.

13

Consolidating Civil War Hospitals at Clarysville

When the Indiana Zouaves arrived in Cumberland in June 1861, they attracted a lot of attention from the residents and understandably so. Hundreds of the soldiers arrived at one time wearing brightly colored uniforms.

Another group of soldiers began arriving around the same time. These men didn't march down Baltimore Street in groups to display themselves. They arrived by train and wagon, even canal boat, at all hours of the day and were carried into hotels and warehouse out of public view.

The pageantry of the Civil War had quickly given way to the reality of soldiers who needed treatment. Because of Cumberland's location at the nexus of the Baltimore and Ohio Railroad, Chesapeake and Ohio Canal, and National Road, it became an ideal location to concentrate medical services. The wounded could be taken from the battlefronts by wagon and driven to Cumberland or loaded onto rail car that would speed them on their way there.

Once in Cumberland, military doctors, local physicians, Catholic sisters and volunteers took care of their needs.

With soldiers facing a much longer recovery time than they do nowadays, the beds in the dozens of temporary hospitals throughout Cumberland filled quickly. More wounded were coming into the city than were being released from the hospitals or buried in the graveyards. Supplies to treat all of them began dwindling.

In March 1862, the *Wheeling Daily Press* published a letter from a Cumberland surgeon thanking the U.S. Sanitary Commission in Wheeling for the supplies that had been sent to Cumberland. The surgeon wrote, in part, "We need them badly and they are doing our soldiers much good. We have about 1200 sick. In consequence of our increasing numbers we have not yet a sufficient supply of bed ticks, comfortable pillows, pillow cases, etc."

Clarysville General Hospital during the Civil War. Courtesy of the Albert and Angela Feldstein Collection.

Besides needing supplies, Surgeon-in-Charge George Suckley wanted to get the wounded out of the drafty warehouses, engine houses and other buildings that were not intended to house people. He began searching for a location where the wounded could be brought that wasn't strung out among two dozen locations throughout Cumberland.

The answer came from an unlikely source.

Mary Townsend came from Frostburg one day to visit her husband who was a local doctor helping care for the wounded soldiers. She sat in Dr. Suckley's office listening to the doctor and her husband discuss the condition of the soldiers as she recounted decades later.

"Can't you think of some place near here where these convalescent men, who are not improving in this dreadful heat, could be transferred?" Dr. Suckley asked Dr. Townsend.

Mrs. Townsend didn't even wait for husband to reply. She said that she knew of a place that was 8.5 miles from Cumberland in a "delightful valley I came through this afternoon with the finest spring water, a large tavern, several houses and three large barns not used for years."

Her description appealed to Dr. Suckley who drove out to Clarysville to see it for himself. "The next day the barns were cleaned and fresh hay put on the floor, then the men were taken up with their blankets and laid on the flood. Many said they had never slept so well, it proved an ideal spot and hundreds of men were saved by the easy transfer," Mrs. Townsend wrote.

Records show that Dr. Suckley, Dr. Townsend and the assistant quartermaster visited Clarysville on March 4, 1862. They liked what they saw and agreed with Mrs. Townsend that the site would make a fine hospital.

Brigade Surgeon John Carpenter wrote later that hospital buildings were "admirably located at a point sufficiently near for comfortable transportation, and sufficiently distant to enjoy all the advantages of a pure atmosphere. The seclusion of the position is such as to allow the convalescent abundant liberty for suitable exercise in the open air, and its purity produces the most admirable tonic effect upon the enfeebled sick. The supply of water is abundant and its quality excellent."

Suckley made arrangements with Rebecca Clary, who owned the property, and Mrs. George Clise, who was renting the property, for the U.S. Government to use it. On March 6, 1862, 100 soldiers helped Mrs. Clise move into a nearby vacant house and the transformation of the inn into a hospital began.

The Clarysville Inn had been built in 1805 and became a popular stop along the National Road. However, it was obvious from the start that the two-story brick inn would not offer sufficient space to bring all of the wounded from Cumberland to Clarysville.

Construction soon began on additional facilities. Within a short time, six wards (150 feet long), three wards (130 feet long), a 100-foot-long ward, a 90-foot-long dining room, a 70-foot-long kitchen, a 38-foot-long storehouse, a 50-foot-long guard quarters, a 44-foot-long bake house and eight waters closets (10 feet long) were built, according to a report written by Capt. George Harrison, assistant quartermaster in 1865.

"These buildings, though well adapted for use in warm weather, do not afford sufficient protection from the cold of winter for sick and wounded men. the declivity of the ground causes them to stand high, the sides are of rough upright boards with crevices not battened to their full height, and the ridge ventilators having no sash to close, the cold wind and snow penetrate to an extant unbearable by the patients," Dr. George Oliver, the surgeon in charge following Dr. Suckley, wrote.

Each ward had two rows of iron cots with an aisle down the center, according to Robert Bruce in *The National Road*.

The influx of wounded continued, though, and even overflowed the capacity of the Clarysville Hospital and filled 15 temporary hospitals in Cumberland and one site in Mount Savage.

The hospital continued serving soldiers until August 1865 when its designation was changed from a General Hospital to Post Hospital. The structure and contents were sold and the government returned the inn to the owners.

The Clarysville Inn remained an operating inn until it burned down on March 10, 1999.

14

The Monitor, The Merrimack and Cumberland

She was a monster; a thing of nightmares. A more-fitting name for the *C.S.S. Virginia* would have been *The Phoenix*, for she had been created from the ashes of the *U.S.S. Merrimack*.

And the *U.S.S. Cumberland*, which had aided in the demise of the *Merrimack,* would help complete the birth of the *Virginia.*

The *Cumberland* was a warship launched in 1842 and converted into a heavy sloop-of-war in 1856. Her armament consisted of 22 nine-inch guns, a 10-inch pivot guns and a Dahlgren rifle gun that fired a 70-pound ball.

When the Civil War began in April 1861, the *Cumberland* was docked at the Gosport Navy Yard in Virginia. Though Virginia had not yet seceded from the Union, its sympathies were with the Confederacy. The day following the bombardment of Fort Sumter, the decision was made to open the underwater valves of the *Merrimack,* another warship, and sink her.

"I begged the captain of the *Cumberland* to withhold the order; for assistance might be sent, and at any time she could be sunk with a shell from our battery. But the order was given, and the *Merrimac* slowly sank till she grounded, with her gun-deck a little out of water," Thomas Selfridge wrote in an 1893 article in *The Cosmopolitan*. He served as a lieutenant on the *Cumberland*.

The next day the order came to abandon the ship yard. Nine ships, or one-quarter of the U.S. Navy according to Selfridge, were burned and an immense amount of weapons and munitions were left behind for the Confederacy.

"It was a splendid, but melancholy spectacle, and in the lurid glare, which turned night into day, the *Cumberland* slipped her moorings, and, in tow of the Pawnee, left Norfolk," wrote Selfridge.

In November, the *Cumberland* sailed to the mouth of the James River near Newport News, but in the interim, she had fought in the bombardment and capture of the Hatteras forts. She was the last American frigate to go to battle under sail.

Topside on the Monitor. Courtesy of the Library of Congress.

By this time, reports had made their way north that the Confederacy had raised the *Merrimack* and were turning her into an ironclad fighting ship. The Union was scurrying to build its own ironclad, but the Confederacy had a head start.

Hampton Roads, where the *Cumberland* was stationed was the entrance to the Chesapeake Bay and from there the gateway to both the capital of the Union and the Confederacy. Union officials feared what the *Merrimack*, now rechristened the *Virginia* would do if made its way to Washington. Navy Secretary Gideon Welles ordered fleet commanders to send ships in Hampton Roads out of harm's way. "The blockade commanders couldn't get the ships out of the Roads in time, and on March 8, a clearly rattled Welles reversed the order. By now, it was too late. His worst nightmare was unfolding," wrote Paul Clancy in his book *Ironclad*.

As the *Virginia*, steamed toward Hampton Roads, Union shore batteries shelled it and watched in amazement as the shells bounced off the iron hull.

The *Cumberland's* crew sighted the *Virginia* around 12:30 p.m. March 8. At first she was believed to be a mirage because of atmospheric conditions.

Monitor Executive Officer Dana Greene

The *Virginia* steamed full speed toward the *Cumberland*. As it passed the *U.S.S. Congress*, it fired a broadside damaging the frigate. Then the *Virginia* rammed the *Cumberland* with a 1500-pound iron spar. Even as the ram sunk deep into the *Cumberland* under the waterline, the *Virginia* reversed its engines. The ram broke off inside the *Cumberland*.

The *Cumberland's* crew fired upon the ship. "So furious was the *Cumberland's* response that the greased sides of the Confederate battery seemed to fry like bacon," wrote Clancy.

Protected by its iron skin, the *Virginia's* guns tore up the crew and deck on the *Cumberland*. Yet, the *Cumberland's* gunners continued firing until the guns slipped underwater.

Selfridge wrote of the crew, "They really believed themselves invincible, and indeed could they have had a fair fight would have shown themselves to be such. With but few officers, for the first time in their lives exposed to a terrible shell fire, seeing their comrades mangled and dead before them. The manner in which these decimated guns' crews stood unflinchingly at their guns, with water pouring over the decks, the ship trembling in the last throes of her disappearance, until the word was passed from their officers, 'Every man look out for himself,' just before the ship went down, was not only sublime, but ought to embalm the name *'Cumberland'* in the heart of every American."

The Confederate Ironclad Merrimack. Courtesy of the Library of Congress.

Seeing the fate of the *Cumberland*, the *Congress* moved into shallower water where the *Virginia* couldn't follow. However, the *Congress* ran aground leaving the *Virginia* free to draw as close as it could and fire upon it until the *Congress* flew the white flag of surrender.

When Confederate boats approached the *Congress*, Union shore batteries fired upon them so the *Virginia* fired incendiary shells at the *Congress* and burned her to the waterline.

It seemed almost too easy. It had been two warships against one new, untested ship. Yet the one had triumphed with no loss of life while the *Cumberland* had sunk with 121 lives of 376 lost and the *Congress* had been burned with 240 dead out of 434.

Nothing could stand in the way of the *Virginia*. It could steam up the Potomac River and bombard Washington or make its way up the coastline to destroy New York Harbor. It was unstoppable.

But even as the crew of the *Virginia* celebrated victory, one ship had heard the sounds of battle and even now steamed south where among the debris of battle. A David would challenge the new Goliath.

Executive Office Dana Greene was born in Cumberland. Courtesy of Wikimedia Commons.

Greene accepts the burden of command

The crew of the *U.S.S. Monitor* wasn't sure what they would find when they steamed into Hampton Roads on March 8, 1862. The sounds of thunder they had heard were now believed to be the sounds of cannon booming during a great battle.

The crew suspected what the *C.S.S. Virginia* could do, but the report sounded like tall tales. An iron hull that the largest cannonball only bounced off of? A ram that would sink a warship in a single blow?

Impossible. Yet this was a new age, an age in which iron could float and, as the crew was about to discover, fable could become fact.

"As we approached Hampton Roads we could see the fine old *Congress* burning brightly, and soon a pilot came on board and told of the arrival of the *Merrimac*, the disaster to the *Cumberland* and the *Congress*, and the dismay of the Union forces," Monitor Executive Officer Samuel Dana Greene wrote in an article in *The Century Magazine* in 1885.

Born in Cumberland, Greene had entered the navy as an "acting midshipman" in 1855 at the age of 15. He volunteered for duty on the *Monitor* and because of the shortage of junior officers in the navy, he was made executive officer. Greene's assigned crewmen to their watches and quarters. He was also gunnery officer and trained the crew on the two Dahlgrens guns in the turret.

The *U.S.S. Minnesota* had been headed to assist the *U.S.S. Cumberland* and the *U.S.S. Congress* in their losing battles against the ironclad *Virginia*, resurrected from the sunken *U.S.S. Merrimack*. The *Monitor* dropped anchor beside the *Minnesota* to give the wooden ship the protection of the Union's hastily built ironclad.

In August 1861, the Navy Department had solicited ideas for ironclad vessels and selected John Ericsson's unique design. The ship had been built in less than 100 days. When in the water, the ship's deck rode only a foot above the water. One Confederate naval officer described the *Monitor* as a cheese box on a shingle.

Early tests of the ship's abilities hadn't been heartening, but it was the Union's only hope to stand against the *Virginia* which had so easily proved victorious over two wooden ships on March 8.

"Between 1 and 2 A. M. the *Congress* blew up, not instantaneously, but successively; her powder-tanks seemed to explode, each shower of sparks rivaling the other in its height, until they appeared to reach the zenith -- a grand but mournful sight. Near us, too, lay the *Cumberland* at the bottom of the river, with her silent crew of brave men, who died while fighting their guns to the water's edge, and whose colors were still flying at the peak," Greene wrote.

The Battle of the Monitor and Merrimack. Courtesy of the U.S. Naval Historical Center.

The Confederate sailors celebrated their victory throughout the night and in the morning, headed toward the *Minnesota* to sink it as well. The *Virginia* came within a mile of the *Minnesota* and opened fire.

The *Monitor* moved alongside the *Virginia*, swiveled its turret so the twin guns faced the *Virginia* and Captain John Worden ordered, "Commence firing!"

"I triced up the port, ran out the gun, and, taking deliberate aim, pulled the lockstring. The *Merrimac* was quick to reply, returning a rattling broadside (for she had ten guns to our two), and the battle fairly began. The turret and other parts of the ship were heavily struck, but the shots did not penetrate; the tower was intact, and it continued to revolve. A look of confidence passed over the men's faces, and we believed the *Merrimac* would not repeat the work she had accomplished the day before," Greene wrote.

As the gunnery officer, he personally chose the target and fired each shot from the *Monitor*.

The *Virginia* wasn't prepared to fight another ironclad. Its guns were loaded with grape shot and explosive shells, which had no effect on an ironclad. Meanwhile the *Monitor* was firing 168-pound balls from 17,000-pound guns.

Captain Henry Van Brunt of the *Minnesota* wrote, "Gun after gun was fired by the *Monitor*, which was returned by whole broadsides from the rebels with no more effect, apparently, than so many pebble stones thrown by a child."

The intense firing caused so much smoke that spectators couldn't see the battle at times. The smaller *Monitor* would move in close to the *Virginia*, sometimes even touching the other ship, and fire both guns. Then the *Monitor* could quickly move to a new location, swivel the turret to redirect the guns and fire again.

Inside the turret, the men, including Greene, were black with powder and nearly deaf from the sound of hits against the iron skin of turret. The turret took at least nine direct hits with the worst damage being dents.

At one point, the *Monitor* tried to ram the *Virginia*, but a steering malfunction caused the *Monitor* to barely miss it. In the pilot house, Worden was looking out when the *Virginia* fired on the passing *Monitor* and hit the pilot house.

Blinded, the captain was carried to a sofa and Greene was called from the turret. Greene arrived and saw the captain. "He was a ghastly sight, with his eyes closed and the blood apparently rushing from every pore in the upper part of his face. He told me that he was seriously wounded, and directed me to take command. I assisted in leading him to a sofa in his cabin, where he was tenderly cared for by Doctor Logue, and then I assumed command," Greene wrote.

Uncertain of how badly the steering gear had been damaged, Greene ordered the *Monitor* to break off the fighting. When Greene found the damage was not so serious that the *Monitor* couldn't fight, the ship reentered the engagement. However, the *Virginia* was itself retreating from the battlefield in order to keep from being trapped by a low tide.

"We of the *Monitor* thought, and still think, that we had gained a great victory. This the Confederates have denied. But it has never been denied that the object of the *Merrimac* on the 9th of March was to complete the destruction of the Union fleet in Hampton Roads, and that in this she was completely foiled and driven off by the *Monitor* nor has it been denied that at the close of the engagement the *Merrimac* retreated to Norfolk, leaving the *Monitor* in possession of the field," Greene wrote.

The destruction of the U.S. Navy Yard at Norfolk that gave the Confederates the U.S.S. Virginia, which became the C.S.S. Merrimack. Courtesy of the U.S. Navy Historical Center.

Davy Jones claims his prize

The nature of naval warfare had changed in the morning of March 9, 1862. The *C.S.S. Virginia* had retreated leaving two destroyed wooden warships behind, but also a victorious ironclad called the *U.S.S. Monitor*.

Because of the battle fought at Hampton Roads, Virginia, the world's wooden navies had become obsolete.

During the battle, Cumberland-born Samuel Dana Greene had commanded the turret of the *Monitor* as executive officer. He had chosen the targets and fired each round. When Captain John Worden had been wounded, the 22-year-old Greene had been given command of the Union ironclad.

Worden wrote of Greene in his report to the Secretary of the Navy, "Lieutenant Greene, the executive officer, had charge in the turret, and handled the guns with great courage, coolness, and skill; and throughout the engagement, as in the equipment of the vessel and on her passage to Hampton Roads, he exhibited an earnest devotion to duty unsurpassed in my experience."

When Worden gave Greene command of the *Monitor*, Greene had moved the ship to shallow water to determine whether it could continue fighting. When the *Monitor* moved back into action, the *Virginia* was already moving toward Norfolk. Rather than pursue, Greene had returned to protect the *U.S.S. Minnesota*, which had been its primary duty.

The next morning as the *Monitor* moved through fleet. "Cheer after cheer went up from the Frigates and small craft for the glorious *Monitor*, and happy indeed did we all feel," Greene wrote.

Later the crew received a hero's welcome in Washington City and a visit from President Abraham Lincoln and Secretary of War Edwin Stanton.

To the Union, the victory was clear; the *Virginia* had abandoned the battlefield. That traditionally meant the *Monitor* was victorious. However, the South refused to admit the loss. They claimed that when Greene pulled away to check the steering gear during the battle, the *Monitor* had retreated and the *Virginia* had then chosen to leave to keep from being trapped by the low tide.

On March 10, Greene was relieved of command because he was thought to be too young and inexperienced to serve as captain. Greene remained with the ship as the executive officer.

The two ironclads would never meet in battle again. Only two months later, with Union troops advancing on Norfolk, the *Virginia* could retreat no further up the James River because the water was too shallow. She was order grounded and blown up to keep from being captured.

The *Monitor's* fate was no better. "We returned to Hampton Roads in November, and sailed thence in tow of the steamer *Rhode Island,* bound for Beaufort, N. C. Between 11 P. M. and midnight on the following night the *Monitor* went down in a gale, a few miles south of Cape Hatteras. Four officers and twelve men were drowned, forty-nine people being saved by the boats of the steamer. It was impossible to keep the vessel free of water, and we presumed that the upper and lower hulls thumped themselves apart," Greene wrote.

Greene was ordered to the *U.S.S. Florida* as executive officer and later transferred to the *U.S.S. Iroquois*. Following the war, he served as an instructor at the Naval Academy.

Though he had a successful career, his failure to sink the *Virginia* and the Confederacy's unwillingness to admit the defeat of the *Virginia* seemed to haunt him. In 1885, Greene wrote a lengthy article about his experience on the *Monitor* and shortly before it was published, he committed suicide by shooting himself.

However, history remembers Greene better than he remembered himself. In 1918, the Navy launched the *U.S.S. Greene*, which would serve until the end of WWII.

In 2002, the *Monitor's* turret and other artifacts, including the remains of two of the lost seamen, were recovered in a Navy salvage operation and are on display in the *U.S.S. Monitor* Center in the Mariner's Museum in Newport News, Virginia.

The Battle of the Monitor and Merrimack. Courtesy of *AmericanCivilWar.com*.

15

A Reporter's View of Cumberland During the War

As the Civil War progressed, reporters from the major newspapers of the day sent reporters trailing after the various armies to report on the fighting from the battlefront. One of the *New York Times'* reporters stayed in Cumberland as he traveled westward along the Baltimore and Ohio Railroad.

He turned in a report of his time in Cumberland that was published in the May 12, 1862, *New York Times*. The reported had been written more than a week earlier near the beginning of May.

In the midst of a war, the reporter showed a strong appreciation of the beauty of the area. "Even in this mountainous section of the country, which usually is far behind the seasons of lower latitudes, the ground is carpeted with verdure, and the little flowers peer forth from their nooks between the rocks, reminding one that the Spring-time is verging into Summer," he wrote.

Clues in the article suggest that he was staying in Revere House next to the railroad. From his room, he described Cumberland this way: "Below me stands the town, compactly built of brick and wood, somewhat irregular, yet with its irregularity beautifully located. A quaint-looking brick church towers above all other buildings, situated on a high hill, with tall spire and gilt cross, looking heavenward, while beneath it a number of white-dwelling-houses cluster as if safe in its fancied protection."

He said the people of Cumberland were quiet, orderly and courteous. Although the city was in Maryland, he noted the mixed loyalties of the people and wrote that he believed that a slight majority might be leaning towards the Confederate States in their loyalties.

A Union soldier camp at Cumberland during the Civil War. From the Herman and Stacia Miller Collection courtesy of the Mayor and City Council of Cumberland, Md.

In one instance, he had an uncomfortable meeting with such a family. On his explorations of the area, the reporter stopped at a house about two miles outside of Cumberland. He knocked on the door and asked the middle-aged woman who answered if he could have a cup of water.

"You're a Yankee, are you not?" the woman asked somewhat brusquely.

The reporter admitted that he was.

"You Northern men will meet with a judgment for freeing those negroes in the District of Columbia. You are all alike—all abolitionists, and if you do conquer us now, we will arise again, and yet be acknowledged free and sovereign states."

The reporter wrote that he tried to convince the woman of her error, but she was not to be reasoned with. Her husband finally came to the door, wondering what was happening. He had a more-mild tone and invited the reporter into the house.

While not a fancy home, the main room did have a piano in it with a "lot of secesh songs" propped up on it. He asked the couple's daughter who was in the room if she would play him a song. The girl played and sung him "Maryland, My Maryland."

"The music of this wonderful song was about equal in composition to the poetical part of it," the reporter wrote.

In Cumberland itself, the reporter noted that martial feel of the city with its many sentries posted all around.

"Sentries have now become an 'institution; among us," he wrote. "At first they were the wonder of small boys and envious countrymen, but since the war is continued, even the small boys have stopped irritating them and parading up and down the walks with sticks, calling out 'left, left,' etc. Now they look at the soldier with *nonchalance*, singing out, in a teasing manner, 'Soldier, won't you work?' while the countryman passes them by as if an ordinary man, so habituated has custom made us to the 'pomp, pride and circumstance of war.'"

Gen. Benjamin Kelley was also in command of the Union troops in the area at this time. The reporter wrote, "I saw him at the station yesterday, and his health is improving fast, but he still suffers from the effects of his wounds."

The reporter spent only a few days in the city before once again boarding the train and heading off toward Wheeling, Va.

16

The Battle of Antietam

The bloodiest single day of the Civil War took place in Washington County during the Battle of Antietam. Nearly 23,000 soldiers were killed, wounded or missing during the fight that ended Confederate General Robert E. Lee's first invasion of Maryland.

Following fighting on South Mountain between Washington and Frederick counties, the Confederate Army moved westward towards Sharpsburg. Then on Sept. 17, the Union and Confederate armies met again on a more-open battlefield outside of Sharpsburg.

The *Hagerstown Herald of Freedom and Torch Light* described the devastation of the battle this way: "Corn and stubble, pasture and fallow contribute their boundaries to the one great charnel house of the nation's host, and on hill, in hollow, through field are strewn the bleeding, mangled bodies of dead and dying humanity. Here our lines stretched over a space of five miles, extending, on the extreme right, from near the intersection of the new and old roads to Sharpsburg, in an easy curve to the south-east, to where the left of Burnside rested at the foot of Elk Ridge Mountain. "

Though the fighting during the day wasn't taking place in the towns of Sharpsburg, Boonsboro and Keedysville, soldiers were moving through the towns while the civilians who hadn't evacuated tried to hide from stray bullets and shells.

Jacob McGraw of Sharpsburg was feeding his horse when the morning barrage started. A Union shell burst over his head sending shrapnel through his barn roof. McGraw wrote that it "came might near gettin' me...It stunned me right smart." He retreated to a neighbor's cellar for safety.

The Confederate soldiers realized that the civilians were in danger and warned them that they needed to leave. It started a mad rush out of town.

Burnside bridge where units of the Union Army struggled to cross Antietam Creek during the Battle of Antietam. Courtesy of the Library of Congress.

"Narrow souled men were seen nailing up their cellars and smoke house door to prevent starved soldiers from taking advantage of their absence and helping themselves to something to eat. ... I saw middle aged women running through the streets literally dragging their children after them; the little fellows had to take such tremendous strides that it seemed to me they hit the ground but seldom. Then came a dozen young ladies, each with a stuffed sack under each arm, some of which in their haste they had forgotten to tie, and as they ran the unmentionables were scattered behind them," one Rebel soldier wrote.

The fighting between the armies stopped at nightfall as both sides began to assess their situations. Civilians also began poking their heads out of their basements to see if they had a house.

"Night came on and permission was asked by the rebels and granted to bury the dead and care for the wounded. Heap upon heap lay piled the dead and wounded. In one field where their advance was checked lay 1,217 rebel dead, while on the hill beyond a number nearly as great of our own men were left to the mercy of the enemy," the *Herald of Freedom and Torch Light* reported.

While the armies could move on to their next battles, their dead and wounded was left for the civilians to deal with. Nearly every house and large building from south of Hagerstown to the Potomac River was filled with wounded soldiers. Others were shipped out to hospitals in Hagerstown and Frederick among other places using Medical Director Jonathan Letterman's new battlefield developments, triage and ambulances.

"The whole region of country between Boonsboro and Sharpsburg is one vast hospital. Houses and Barns are filled with them, and nearly the whole population is engaged in waiting on and ministering to their wants. In this town the Washington House, County Hall, and Lyceum Hall have been appropriated to the use of the wounded, and our citizens, especially the ladies, are untiring in their efforts to relieve them," reported the *Herald of Freedom and Torch Light*.

Residents were also left wondering about how they would get by given how badly the battle had devastated the area.

"The region of country between Sharpsburg and Boonsboro' has been eaten out of food of every description. The two armies of from eighty to a hundred thousand each have swept over it, and devoured everything within reach. At Sharpsburg, we understand that the rebels sacked the town, and when they left many of the citizens had not a morsel of food to eat," according to the *Herald of Freedom and Torch Light*.

Though the Battle of Antietam is considered a draw militarily, it gave President Abraham Lincoln the political impetus to be able to issue the Emancipation Proclamation that declared slaves in Confederate States to be free. This changed the goal of the war from a political war over states' rights to a moral one to abolish slavery.

17

A Confederate Post Office in Cumberland

Though Cumberland remained in the Union during the Civil War, it doesn't mean that everyone supported the Union. However, Confederate sympathizers had to keep their feelings hidden or they might wind up in prison. Also, given that there were as many soldiers in the city as there were residents, it was hard to say something without a soldier being near who could report them.

Still, as the old saying goes, "Where there's a will, there's a way."

One of the needs that sympathizers had was finding a way to communicate with their sons who had gone off to fight for the Confederate States.

Though Cumberland had had a post office since 1795 when Charles F. Broadhag was appointed Postmaster, Confederate sympathizers couldn't walk to the post office and mail a letter to a state that the Union was fighting against.

According to Robert C. Moody in his article, "A Confederate Post Office in Kentucky," Federal post offices were often located in the postmaster's home during the Civil War.

When the Civil War first broke out in April 1861, the U.S. Post Office continued delivering mail in the Confederate States for another seven weeks.

"Mail that was postmarked after the date of a state's admission into the Confederacy through May 31, 1861, and bearing US (Union) postage is deemed to represent 'Confederate State Usage of U.S. Stamps'," Moody wrote.

After that initial grace period, private express companies were then used to carry the mail across enemy lines. This continued for about two months until the U.S. government ordered it to end on August 26, 1861.

Following this, sympathizers began creating unofficial post offices that essentially operated as smuggling hubs with the contraband being smuggled letters and supplies.

A Confederate States of America postage stamp featuring President Jeff Davis.

Though there were probably other Confederate post offices in Allegany County during the war, the best-known one was run out of a business on Baltimore Street throughout the length of the war.

"Back in Cumberland, those ladies whose hearts were with the South operated a secret Confederate Post Office in the rear of a Baltimore Street store; they donated money, food, and clothing to Confederate prisoners passing through the city headed for prison camps in

Ohio; and they served as informants for the guerilla unites operating in the South Branch Valley," Michael Allen Mudge wrote in *The McKaig Journal: A Confederate Family of Cumberland*.

No stamps were sold from these Confederate post offices and because of the short time these post offices existed and their secretive nature, few records exist of their existence and thus, little is known about them.

Based on what is known about how these post offices operated in other areas, Confederate couriers would bring mail into Cumberland to the post office. It might be marked with the person's name and "Cumberland, Maryland." Once delivered to the store on Baltimore Street, the mail would quickly be dispatched to the recipients by other sympathizers.

"In most cases, this manner of mail distribution was the only way information could get from the southern battlefields to the soldiers' family members in this area," Moody wrote.

18

Clarysville Hospital Doctor Faces Court Martial

Charles Fosdick watched the man stagger about the hospital, stumbling, shuffling, pausing occasionally to lean against something to regain his balance. Fosdick frowned and shook his head. It wasn't a patient under the influence of a medication whom he was watching. This many was the ranking surgeon for both of the military hospitals in Clarysville and Cumberland. He was a doctor, an officer and a drunk.

Fosdick was a member of the U.S. Sanitary Commission who was touring the western Maryland hospitals. And what Fosdick was seeing he didn't like.

The commission was a government agency created in 1861 to coordinate the efforts of women who wanted to volunteer and help with the Union war effort. The volunteers raised money, provided nursing services, cooked in camps, ran hospital ships and soldiers' homes, made uniforms and more.

When Fosdick returned home to Ohio after his hospital tour, the memory of what he had seen disturbed him so much that he wrote to the Honorable J.R. Gurley and explained how he had visited the hospital on a Saturday night and found the ranking surgeon, Major George Oliver, drunk "so much so he was entirely incompetent for duty under any circumstance." Upon investigation of the incident, Fosdick had heard numerous stories that Oliver treated the sick roughly and was drunk much of the time.

Other letters began to reach officials in Washington about Oliver's behavior. They all told stories similar to Fosdick's.

It wasn't the first time that Oliver had run into problems. In 1862, he had been serving in Wheeling, Virginia. His superior, Dr. Jonathan

Letterman wrote the U.S. Surgeon General saying that Oliver's habits should keep him from holding a position of responsibility in a hospital.

As a result, Oliver was transferred to Cumberland where he served under Brigade Surgeon George Suckley. However, when Suckley was transferred, Oliver became the ranking medical officer.

While complaints began to mount against Oliver, he still managed some accomplishments. He consolidated the hospitals in Cumberland to Clarysville and was able to manage the care of nearly 1,100 soldiers.

Surgeon J. Simpson was asked to examine the charges against Oliver in January 1863. Simpson reported later, "There appears to be no foundation for accusations of incompetency or neglect."

The Clarysville Inn that served as the center of a Civil War hospital compound in Allegany County. Courtesy of *Whilbr.org*.

However, the accusations persisted and in April 21, 1863, a court martial trial was convened in Cumberland to fully examine the charges against Oliver. The surgeon was charged with five counts of violation of the 45th Article of War – being drunk on duty, one count of conduct unbecoming an officer and gentleman, two counts of neglect of duty, two counts of neglect of duty, prejudicial to good order and military discipline.

As testimony progressed, one interesting turn was that Dr. Morris Townsend testified that it wasn't liquor that incapacitated Oliver but neuralgia and rheumatism. "I frequently endeavored to discharge duties for him rather than see him attending to them when he was incompetent by physical suffering. One effect of the disease under which he labored was to produce an irregularity, an uncertainty of gait and movement for which I knew the cause better than anyone else, having had to treat him for those disease," Townsend testified.

Much of the testimony was conflicting as both sides produced officers who told conflicting stories of the same incidents.

After about two weeks of testimony, Oliver was found not guilty of all charges. However, the court martial board did find that Oliver wasn't forwarding paperwork properly to headquarters. This was not a chargeable offense, though.

In August, Oliver left the area when he was transferred west at his own request in the hopes that the dry climate would help his rheumatism. However, by September 1864, he was once again facing possible charges. He resigned rather than face them.

19

The Day Cumberland Was in the Confederacy

Cumberlanders had been frightened at times during the Civil War. At the beginning of the conflict, residents of the Western Maryland city had feared a Southern invasion. Merchants had barricaded their stores. The local militia was called out to the city limit to present a protective line. All of this was in response to a rumor that "a large band of lawless persons from some direction" was marching on Cumberland to take the city.[1]

A few months later in August 1861, a crowd gathered on Baltimore Street in downtown Cumberland to hear Francis Thomas promote the Union cause. When Confederate sympathizers heckled him, the gathering turned into a riot between pro-Union and pro-Confederate residents.

Yet, except for a few months at the beginning of the war, the Union Army was always present to give the citizens some sense of safety; to be their wall against the Confederate Army. At times, the number of Union soldiers in the area matched the number of residents in the city.

On June 10, 1861, residents had awakened to find soldiers dressed in uniforms of contrasting red, blue and gray marching into the city. The continued through Cumberland and made their camp on high ground north of the city in the shadow of Haystack Mountain.

These were the 11th Indiana Regiment in their Zouave uniforms and commanded by Colonel Lew Wallace.[2] The Zouave units in the war were based on North African soldiers and known for their elaborate and colorful uniforms. Cumberland was their first duty station outside of Indiana since the unit had been organized in April 1861.

Wallace created a strong relationship between the residents and his men. Concerts and marches entertained the citizenry. However, despite these friendly relations, secessionist sentiment was not tolerated in the region. Southern sympathizers were rounded up and made to swear an oath of allegiance to the United States. Some were exiled from the city. Others, including State Senator Thomas J. McKaig, served time in federal prisons for voicing their opinions.

While Cumberland might have been a Union city, it was an occupied Union city and the omnipresent soldiers made that evident to the citizens.

Wallace and the Zouaves moved out of the city in July 1861, but two Pennsylvania regiments filled their vacant camp.

Other generals followed Wallace, including Robert F. Shenck, Benjamin F. Kelley, George C. Crook and Franz Siegel. They all made Cumberland a Union stronghold and it remained that way until the troops mustered out in the summer of 1865.

That's what made June 17, 1863 so different.

It was the day Cumberland fell to the Confederacy.

The jitters

Despite the size of the Union Army in Cumberland, Confederate forces continued to roam the area and inflict damage on the Baltimore and Ohio Railroad, which the Union forces attempted to keep open from the railroad's hub in Cumberland. Particularly worrisome was Romney, West Virginia, which continued to move back and forth between Confederate and Union forces and would do so more than 50 times during the war. The city was less than 30 miles from Cumberland. From that point, Confederate forces could and did move against the B&O Railroad, burning bridges and tearing up track.

As the Union Army grew in numbers, Secretary of War Edwin Stanton recommended that the District of Cumberland be formed. The district was organized in March 1862 with three regiments of infantry and one cavalry troop, totaling about 2,900 men. In addition, the Second Regiment, Potomac Home Guard served in the area.

Yet, a strong Confederate sentiment remained in the area bubbling beneath the coat of blue on the city.

Some men left the city to join Confederate units elsewhere in Maryland or headed across the Potomac River to find a unit. "And whenever a Confederate raiding party appeared in the vicinity, the next few issues of the newspapers would not that several youngsters were missing from the homes and presumed to have joined the rebels."[3]

An underground mail service to get messages to rebels operated out of a store on Baltimore Street throughout the war. [4] Railroad bridges across the Potomac River had a short life span as Confederate force or Confederate sympathizers destroyed them.

On Sunday, June 14, 1863, Maj. General Robert Milroy's command at Winchester, Va. "had been attacked, overpowered, and cut to pieces by Confederate forces under Lieutenant General Richard S. Ewell."[5] Ewell's forces captured 4,000 prisoners, but some, including Milroy escaped. A few men made it to Cumberland to spread the news and worry the citizens.

Leaving the city

Cumberland was a strategic location throughout the war. As the terminus of the Chesapeake and Ohio Canal, it was a main route for getting coal into Washington D.C. Cumberland was also a major hub for the B&O Railroad. It was also a gateway to through the mountains and to the west along the National Road.

The Confederates never seemed to realize the importance of the city to the defense of the Union or if they did, it was after the Union Army had already entrenched itself in the area.

That changed in June 1863.

On Monday, June 15, the troops in Cumberland received orders "to evacuate and report to New Creek."[6] Maj. General Robert Schenck, commanding the Middle Department from his headquarters in Baltimore, sent a message to Maj. General W.T. H. Brooks, commander of the Department of the Monongahela, Pittsburgh, Pennsylvania, saying, "I have ordered all troops I have on the B&O Railroad, and also those of Brigadier General Averill's brigade south of the road, to concentrate, as far as practicable, under General Kelley's command, at New Creek, or some other point on the road, at his discretion, where he can best prevent the rebel force from going westward…" [7]

The Union forces were gathering to oppose General Robert E. Lee and the Army of Northern Virginia, which was expected to push into Maryland for an offensive assault. General G. K. Warren, chief engineer of the defending Army of the Potomac considered Lee's most-likely ford across the river at Greenspring, West Virginia, southeast of Cumberland. This would have made Cumberland an easy target for an invading army.

While General Lee did cross into Maryland, the crossing was made at Williamsport, Maryland, about 60 miles east of Cumberland, as the Confederates marched on their way north toward Pennsylvania where history would be made in Gettysburg.

Preparations for the movement of troops from Cumberland to New Creek took place quickly. "In a short time droves of horses, trains of heavily loaded wagons, etc, were in motion, bound for New Creek. The railroad company, also, as a precautionary matter, removed all their rolling stock, metal tools, etc."[8]

On Tuesday, June 16th, the 15th Va. Regiment and the 2nd Regiment, Maryland Potomac Home Brigade, both nearby Union forces, also headed toward New Creek leaving Cumberland defenseless for the first time in two years.

Not only had the Union troops pulled out of Cumberland and headed south, but the B&O Railroad moved its equipment and material north into Pennsylvania to keep it from Southern hands. While there was no immediate danger of an invasion, without troops to guard the city, invasion became a very real possibility.

With no military defense, the city residents were hysterical, expecting the Confederate Army to march on them at any time.

"On the 16th, it was reported that the enemy was rapidly approaching the city in force, whereupon a number of citizens retired with considerable precipitancy in the direction of Pennsylvania, and merchants began to cast about for means whereby they might save their goods from confiscation by unexpected visitors," James Thomas and Thomas Williams wrote in the *History of Allegany County*.[9]

Yet, night fell and Cumberland remained untaken.

Cumberland surrenders

Gen. Kelley and his staff arrived in Cumberland from Harpers Ferry at 3:30 a.m. on the June 17. At 6 a.m., he and his men then headed by train for New Creek to join with the massing Union Army, but they found the railroad track torn up about 10 miles outside of Cumberland.

Kelley and his staff "Returned to Cumberland and found the place invested by Imboden with two regiments of cavalry and battery. On the outside of town, I met Lieutenant James P. Hart, of the Ringgold Battalion, with 50 cavalry, under whose escort, I, with staff, came here," Kelley wrote to Schenck after his arrival in New Creek.[10]

Later that morning, residents awoke and saw the rebels and artillery pieces on Williams Road east of the city. Two cavalrymen with Ringgold's Battalion approached the rebels and were fired upon. The cannon shells missed the cavalrymen and landed near McKaig's foundry. The cavalrymen quickly retreated back to the city.

The shots only confirmed the fears of the citizens. Frightened citizens took refuge and merchants closed up their stores. Other groups of citizens gathered in the street to see what would happen.[11]

Shortly thereafter, two Confederates entered town and rode on horseback down Baltimore Street under the white flag of truce. Acting Mayor Valentine A. Buckey (who was actually the ranking city councilman at the time) and a group of citizens met them under a flag of truce.

The Confederate soldiers handed Buckey a note addressed to the military commander of Cumberland from Colonel George W. Imboden of the 18th Virginia Cavalry. He served under Brigadier General John D. Imboden, who was also his brother.

The letter read: "You are surrounded by a superior force, and as an act of humanity, I demand the surrender of the city. The bearer, Captain R.B. Muses, is authorized to negotiate as to terms of surrender."[12]

Buckey read the letter, consulted with the other citizens in his group and wrote out his reply. He gave it to Muses to take back to Imboden. His letter to Imboden read: "Sir: Your note addressed to officer commanding at this point has just been handed to me, and as there is no force here to resist you, and no officer in command, I, as Mayor, for the time being, do as far as I can, surrender the city as demanded, upon the following terms, viz: That private persons and property, and the property of the State of Maryland, be respected."[13]

Imboden's written reply was: "Sir: I will receive a surrender of the City of Cumberland, and will respect all private property except such property as the Quartermaster may desire for the Confederate States. No public property except of the State of Maryland will be respected."[14]

About 350 of Imboden's Cavalry took possession of Cumberland. Their first priority was to secure fresh horses. The soldiers and convinced the merchants to open their stores.[15]

"The Confederates then purchased pretty freely such articles as hats, boots, shoes, clothing, etc., paying for the same in Confederate money, a species of currency which had then rather limited value," wrote Thomas and Williams.[16]

While the soldiers respected most property, they did tear down the telegraph lines and remove train track. The railroad depot and machine shops were left untouched.

The Valley News Echo reported, "The conduct of the Confederates throughout was gentlemanly. They were well-clothed, armed and mounted, and exhibited in no respect evidence of starvation or raggedness."[17]

The Confederates knew a substantial Union force was in New Creek so they remained in Cumberland for only three hours, leaving by 10:30 a.m. They crossed to the Potomac River at Greenspring, then continued onto Paw Paw, West Virginia and Bloomery Gap.

When they left the city, a few residents who were sympathetic to the Southern cause also went with them. Among these young men were Thomas Black, Lewis Rice and James Thomas. They became members of Company E, a unit of the 18th Virginia Cavalry, according to Harold Scott in *The Civil War Era in Cumberland, Maryland and nearby Keyser, West Virginia (1861-1865)*.[18]

Back under Union protection

Kelley's forces did not arrive back in Cumberland until the next evening, when they were greeted with cheers. In fact, Kelley's soldiers captured a few of Imboden's men who had remained behind to visit with friends in Cumberland awhile longer.[19]

The Union Army also found that the B&O Railroad and the C&O Canal had been damaged. It took more than a month to restore the telegraph communications because the damage Imboden's men had done.

"*The Richmond Enquirer* told of 'millions of dollars worth of damage done at Cumberland; and Baltimore and Pittsburgh papers dolefully announced a great disaster in Cumberland," wrote David Dean in *Allegany County-A History*.[20]

The only casualty of the capture of Cumberland was Griffin Twigg, a farmer who lived near Murley's Branch.

"The particulars are not known, but the old man was killed; not, however, until he had killed two of the enemy and wounded another," William Lowdermilk wrote in *A History of Cumberland, Maryland*.[21]

Scott believes the casualties in that exchange may have been greater. During a project to collect information on old tombstones and grave sites in the county during the 1980's, the Genealogical Society of Allegany County, Md. came across a burial site with five markers. The property, which is in the area of Murley's Branch is called the Jesse Twigg Cemetery. The modern owner reported that the graves belonged to Jesse Twigg and Confederate soldiers who tried to steal his horses during the war.[22]

With the return of the Union forces to Cumberland, things gradually settled down to normal. The B&O Railroad rolling stock was returned from Pennsylvania, stores opened for business and gossip and rumors thrived. However, Cumberland once again escaped serious loss of lives and property in a devastating war.

Modern repercussion

In the 1990's, the Cumberland City Hall had a display in the rotunda of all the flags that had flown over the city, including the Union Jack from the pre-United States days and the Stars and Bars from June 17, 1863. A complaint from the local chapter of the National Association for the Advancement of Colored People caused it to be removed.

20

The Banishment of a Confederate Family

Priscilla McKaig held the military order in her hand and re-read it. It was short but it was impossible. Major General David Hunter, who was in command of the Union forces in Allegany County for a portion of the Civil War, was ordering her and her family to leave Cumberland for one of the Confederate States.

"I was thunder struck, no charges – no explanation," she wrote in her journal.

Why shouldn't she be? Her family was among the upper class of Cumberland. Her husband was a former mayor of Cumberland, a partner in the Cumberland Cotton Factory and president of the Frostburg Coal Company.

Her first reaction was to refuse to comply. This was her family's home and she had every right to be here. However, she had no choice but to comply. Troops ringed her house and she and her family had been given 24 hours to leave. She must leave by 7 p.m. on July 12, 1863.

Unable to sleep that night, she and her family began preparing to leave. They sent household items like linens and silver, away for safekeeping with friends. Other things were considered too valuable to leave behind and too dangerous to take with them in case their belongings were searched by Union troops. So all of Priscilla's letters from her sons and others with Confederate sympathies were burned.

When a soldier called on her in the morning with a pass to get Priscilla and her children through the Union pickets, she once again acted defiant. "I told him that I did not intend to obey that order, that I considered it was a most heartless, cruel order, that it was out of the question for me to think of going. My Husband was absent, my youngest son was away at school, and also my clothes were wet in the tub."

The soldiers also went to the home of Dr. R.S. McKaig, Priscilla's brother-in-law. He and his family had also been ordered south. When the doctor said he would not leave because it would ruin him, he was immediately arrested and sent west to a prison the following morning. Another brother and Maryland state senator, Thomas Jefferson McKaig, had been arrested in a similar fashion at the beginning of the war and imprisoned.

Rather than depress Priscilla McKaig, the event actually gave her hope that her order would not be enforced.

However, later that day, another order was received noting that they had half an hour to load a carriage of their choosing or a conveyance out of town would be chosen for them.

Oddly, only Priscilla and her son, Beall, left. Priscilla's husband William and son, Merwin (though Merwin would join her later), were left behind. Priscilla was accompanied by her sister-in-law, Sarah, and Sarah's two sons.

The first night away from Cumberland was miserable and Priscilla blamed her family's woes on the fact that her nephew had joined McNeill's Rangers against his father's wishes, despite that fact that she had two sons fighting with the Confederate army. She wrote, "Oh, what a miserable night. I did not sleep an hour, here we heard that all the clothes, money and letter I had sent Tommy were captured. All our troubles were brought on by John McKaig's imprudence and disobedience to his Father's instructions."

The group traveled south to Romney and then to Moorefield, staying with friendly families or paying for rooms in a boarding house. During this time, Priscilla continued to write to her sons, William and Tommy, who were serving.

While staying near Moorefield in August, she saw Gen. John McCausland's troops surprised and routed by Union forces. "I never wish to witness another such a scene. The Federals captured between three and four hundred men, all the artillery and a large number of horses."

During their travels they also began to experience the inflation of Confederate currency. At one boarding house, they paid $80 for a night's lodging, supper and breakfast. Breakfast alone was $16 in one location.

Throughout much of their journeys in the Shenandoah Valley, Priscilla also experienced various ailments from headaches, stomachaches and colic. Sometimes they would keep her in bed all day.

Then in October as winter began to set in, they met Billy McKaig in Moorefield. Since she thought he was supposed to be off fighting, it surprised her. However, what surprised her even more was that her nephew said he had come to get her.

"I could not believe that he had come for that purpose, but supposed that he had returned to join the army. I again said to him, what did you come for Billy? He answered the same way and said pulling a paper out of his pocket, 'here is the order for your return' Oh! how thankful I felt to God for his goodness and mercy to me, the carriage was soon surrounded by friends to congratulate me on my good fortune."

They spent a day packing up their belongings and making sure that all their clothes were clean, then they headed toward Cumberland. They arrived around 5 p.m. the next day.

"Oh how thankful I was, once more to see my home and to meet my dead Husband and my friends," she wrote.

She could not return to house immediately, as it was serving to house officers. Instead she drove to her husband's office. At first, she "could see no one for a few moments, the first one who came to meet me was my dear Husband, who was so filled with emotion that he could hardly speak, directly my Sister and others came running down to meet me. I felt very happy and gratified, we went up to her house and remained there all night."

The McKaigs reclaimed their house next day and things slowly got back to normal. However, they would still run into suspicions throughout the remainder of the war. Once, soldiers searched the house thinking to find one of her Confederate sons at home. As the war wound down, Priscilla's concerns were only for the safety of her sons rather than the Confederate cause.

She mentions events like the surrender of Richmond, surrender of General Lee and the assassination of Abraham Lincoln in her journal, but only in a sentence or two and without any emotion pro or con. On her way back to Cumberland from a trip to New York, her train met the Lincoln funeral train. It was the type of event most people would get philosophical about. Not Priscilla. For her, as well as the rest of the country, the war was done.

21

C&O Canal President Imprisoned for Treason

Rule of thumb: Never say anything out loud or in writing that you don't want other people to know. It was a rule that Alfred Spates, president of the C&O Canal during the Civil War, apparently never learned even after he was arrested three times during the war.

When the Civil War started, President Abraham Lincoln had to be pretty heavy handed with Maryland in order to keep the state in the Union. If he hadn't, there's a good chance that Washington D. C. might have found itself in the Confederate States. As part of this heavy-handedness, high-level Confederate sympathizers in Maryland were arrested and imprisoned. Among these was Thomas McKaig, a state senator from Cumberland.

The first time that Spates ran afoul of the Federal government is believed to have been after the September 1862 Battle of Antietam, according to Harlan Unrau in *The Chesapeake and Ohio Canal During the Civil War: 1861-1865*. Spates wasn't arrested but he was detained for questioning.

On July 6, 1863, Spates was trapped in Hagerstown when the Confederate Army retreating from Gettysburg, took control of the city from the Union Cavalry. Spates met with Lt. General Richard Ewell "regarding the damages to the canal, and that he had obtained a pass to cross Confederate lines directly from General Lee," Timothy Snyder wrote in *Trembling in the Balance*.

Later in the month, Spates was in Baltimore and told a group of men he knew that he had visited General Robert E. Lee in Hagerstown. One of the men in the group, William H. Hoffman, reported the story to the Provost Marshal. Hoffman was a former Congressman and treasurer of the Canal Company. Spates believed that Hoffman said something because he wanted to become president of the C&O Canal.

The Provost Marshal questioned Spates and released him. Spates wrote a letter to the Provost Marshal in late August proclaiming his innocence, but he was still rearrested on Sept. 1. Spates posted bond and was released in mid-September.

Confederate soliders raided the C&O Canal during the Civil War. Courtesy of *Harper's Weekly*.

Spates trial before a military tribunal began on Sept. 16 and lasted three weeks. During that time, he was imprisoned in Fort McHenry. The tribunal found him guilty of crossing Confederate lines and communicating with the enemy on December 4, 1863, but Spates was found not guilty of giving aid and intelligence to the enemy. The guilty charge was enough to see him sentenced to spend the rest of the war in the prison at Fort Warren in Boston Harbor.

Spates made an appeal to Assistant Secretary of War Peter Watson in the hopes of getting Secretary of War Edwin Stanton to pardon him. Spates wrote, "I went to Washington County to put the Chesapeake and Ohio Canal in order—and did—for the use of the Government and Genl. Kelly [sic] now here will state I did and he used it."

The appeal worked and Spates' sentence was overturned in January 1864.

Following his release, Spates returned to his position as president of the C&O Canal.

During this time, Spates also served as President of the Cumberland City Bank. Following the war, he served as a Maryland state senator from Allegany County.

22

John Garrett Used the Railroad to Help the Union

The Baltimore and Ohio Railroad was one of the Union's greatest weapons during the Civil War. It wasn't a weapon of destruction but of transportation. The United States had 200 railroads when the war began. Most of them were in the North. Also, the distinctive thing about the Northern railroads was that most of them had a uniform distance between their rails. This allowed the Union to move troops and goods faster and with fewer transfers than the Confederacy could.

Even among the Northern railroads, the B&O was special. At the beginning of the war, the B&O had 513 miles of track that ran from Washington, DC, to Wheeling, Virginia.

"From Wheeling, the train would be taken across the river on floats to Parkersburg," said Courtney Wilson, executive director of the B&O Railroad Museum in Baltimore. From there, connections could be made to other railroads, but the Washington, DC, connection was the critical one. In terms of rail service, the B&O was Washington's lifeline to the Union.

While the right of way of the railroad made it useful for moving troops along the front, part of it ran through areas that at times were under Confederate control. The Confederate troops recognized the advantage the B&O gave the Union and often targeted it for destruction. Over the course of the war, 143 raids and battles involved the B&O.

"Millions and millions and millions of dollars of damage was done to the railroad during the war," Wilson said.

The Union also recognized the importance that keeping the railroad running meant to the war effort. Brigades were station on the eastern and western ends of the rail line and were dedicated to protecting the B&O from not only regular Confederate Army actions, but also raids from the growing number of ranger units.

John Garrett, president of the B&O Railroad during the Civil War. Courtesy of Wikimedia Commons.

Echoes of War Drums

John W. Garrett was president of the B&O during from 1858 until he died in 1884. He was a Virginian by birth and he continued to treasure his birth state even after it seceded from the Union.

"His loyalties were in question at first because he had called the B&O a Southern railroad," Wilson said. He also referred to Confederate leaders as "our Southern friends."

However, Garrett realized that his financial future lay with a Union victory in the war. Once he realized this, Garrett became a staunch Unionist. Besides, allowing the army to transport troops on the railroad, he allowed telegraph lines to be strung along the railroad's right of way to facilitate communication.

His support of the Union could clearly be seen prior to the Battle of Monocacy in 1864. Railroad agents began reporting Confederate troop movements a week and a half before the battle. Garrett passed the information on to Gen. Lew Wallace who was in charge of the Union defense. He also made sure that trains carried munitions and troops to the area.It was a win-win situation for both the railroad and the Union. The Union was able to move its men and equipment quickly to where they were most needed. Garrett got army protection for the railroad and lucrative government contracts.

The B&O went on to play an important role throughout the war from being attacked during John Brown's raid on Harper's Ferry to transporting President Lincoln's body back to Illinois after his assassination.

When Garrett County formed from Allegany County in 1872, the citizenry chose to honor the man who brought the railroad to the region by naming the new county in his honor.

23

Cumberland's Biggest Civil War Battle

Cumberland was going to burn and the residents were in a panic. They rushed around buying supplies, packing their valuables and hiding. Those that could left town. The enemy was coming. A soldier had ridden into Cumberland from Hancock on July 31, 1864, bringing word that a Confederate Army of 2,800 men was approaching. Before the day was out, people were saying that a smaller Confederate force was also approaching the city from Bedford, PA.

The Confederate forces had moved into the north to take revenge on the Union for the burning of farms in the Shenandoah Valley. Brigadier General John McCausland's men had occupied Chambersburg, PA, and demanded a ransom of $100,000 in gold or $500,000 in currency, knowing that the money couldn't be raised. It wasn't and Chambersburg was burned.

After leaving Chambersburg in smoldering ruins, McCausland and his men had marched into Hancock demanding $3,000 or the town of 700 would suffer the same fate as Chambersburg. The townspeople weren't able to raise the funds, but Brigadier General William Averill was in pursuit of McCausland. On July 31, Averill "appeared on the outskirts of the town and dropped several shells" on the Confederate forces outside of Hancock, according to *The War of Rebellion: A Compilation of the Official Records of the Union and Confederate Armies*.

The Confederates pushed the Union Army back and set off on the National Road toward Cumberland. "The Rebs burned all the bridges on the Pike between this place and Flintstone & cut trees across the road..." Hancock merchant James Riley Smith noted in his diary. While this hindered the pursuit of Averill and his men, it also meant that the Confederate forces had only one direction to go. Now it appeared that Cumberland would become the next Chambersburg.

Confederate General John McCausland left Chambersburg, Pa., in ashes before heading toward Cumberland in 1864. Courtesy of the Library of Congress.

"The wildest excitement prevailed throughout the city, and a public meeting was held Sunday night, for the purpose of organizing a militia force to assist the soldiers under command of General Kelly (sic)," William Lowdermilk wrote in *A History of Cumberland, Maryland*.

Cumberland Mayor Charles Ohr led the meeting and urged that the men in the city to form themselves into defensive companies to protect their homes and families. Three companies were eventually formed of about 200 men each and General C. M. Thruston, the previous mayor was placed in command.

Brigadier General Benjamin Kelley took command of a rag-tag

group of roughly 1,600 men. Besides the Cumberland men, 100-days soldiers and worn and shell-shocked soldiers who had been defeated at the Battle of Second Kernstown the previous month made up Kelley's army.

The following day, Kelley ordered his son, Lieutenant Tappen Kelley, to take a cavalry squad east to hinder McCausland's advance on Cumberland and report back on his progress. This would hopefully give the main force more time to prepare a defense.

The 153rd Ohio was sent to Oldtown to destroy the bridge over the Chesapeake and Ohio Canal to keep the Confederates from re-crossing the Potomac River. This left four infantry regiments, a company of cavalry and three sections of artillery with nine guns to defend Cumberland. He led them out to Folck's Mill, which was a family mill owned by John Folck about three miles east of town. Thurston and the Cumberland man were positioned on Williams Road on the right flank. Though Kelley commanded fewer men than McCausland, he had a good defensive position and an artillery advantage.

The residents of Cumberland were making their own preparations for the expected battle. "The excitement now reached fever heat; the merchants loaded their goods and sent them off to places of safety; the railroad companies moved their trains off to the West, and men were rushing about the streets arming themselves with muskets, rifles and shot guns, while thousands climbed to the hill-tops, for the purpose of obtaining a view of the expected conflict," Lowdermilk wrote.

The Confederate soldiers were first sighted around noon when they were six miles outside of town. By 3 p.m., a Confederate cavalry squadron was approaching Folck's Mill. They crossed a covered bridge over Evitt's Creek that brought them into range of the Union artillery.

Kelley's men opened with their artillery fire and the Confederates took cover behind the bridge and mill buildings. They then began to return fire with their four pieces of artillery. Both sides continued to exchange artillery fire, along with sharpshooters on both sides adding their fire.

During the battle, the *Alleganian* reported, "The dwelling, mill and barn of John Folck, Esq., were pretty much in range of our guns and were struck several times by shell.— The barn was fired by an exploding shell, and was entirely destroyed with its contents almost the entire product of the late harvest."

Once night fell, the Confederates retreated to the South to the South to cross the Potomac River at Greenspring Run. They left behind two caissons several carriages and a lot of ammunition.

Casualty reports vary from as many as 60 (30 wounded on each side) to as low as 16 (one Confederate killed, two wounded and 12 Union wounded). More importantly, Cumberland was still intact.

24

Oldtown's Civil War Skirmish

In August 1864, a Confederate force intent on burning Cumberland had been turned away by the combined force of the Union army and local militia. As darkness had fallen on Aug. 1, General John McCausland used the night as cover to pull his men back and retreat towards Oldtown where there was bridge across the Potomac into West Virginia.

The Confederate force of approximately 2,800 men reached Oldtown around 5 a.m. on the morning of Aug. 2, expecting to move quickly across the bridge to the safety on the other side of the river. However, Union General Benjamin Kelley had sent the men of the 153rd Ohio National Guard to defend the crossing the day before. These men were 100-day soldiers. They had burned the bridges across the Chesapeake and Ohio Canal and entrenched themselves between the canal and Potomac River in preparation for a fight.

The Confederate army was stopped at the canal and set to work to build a temporary bridge. Once across the canal, the two groups started firing on each other. Confederate General Bradley Johnson managed to flank the Ohioans and force them to fall back across the Potomac River.

"By the time he had reached the Virginia side, his men had become so demoralized that all but five officers and seventy-seven enlisted men took the cars which had carried them down, and moved out of reach of the enemy," according to *The War of Rebellion: A Compilations of the Official Records of the Union and Confederate Armies.*

With only a small number of men left to command, Col. Israel Stough of the Ohio 153rd repositioned his men near a Union blockhouse in Greenspring, W.Va., where he could get assistance from Capt. Peter Petrie and Company K of the Potomac Home Brigade. Besides the protection of the block house, Petrie also offered the protection an iron-clad train that was equipped with artillery pieces.

Johnson's artillery disabled the train and took out one of the guns in a relatively short time, though. "Captain Petrie's command was compelled to take shelter in the woods, leaving Colonel Stough in the blockhouse," according to the *Official Records*.

Blockhouses like this were used to protect the canal and railroad during the Civil War. Courtesy of the Library of Congress.

The blockhouse lived up to its name, though, and the small group of Union soldiers was able to push back the Confederates each time they advanced. Finally, after an hour and a half stand-off, Johnson wrote out a message demanding the surrender of the blockhouse and sent it to Stough under the protection of a flag of truce.

Stough realized that his position couldn't be held forever outnumbered as he was by nearly 30 to 1, so he agreed to surrender if he and his men would be immediately paroled and left with their personal property and a hand car to use to travel back to Cumberland.

Johnson agreed to the conditions. The Union men left the blockhouse and the Confederate soldiers promptly destroyed it and the armored cars before retreating across the river.

Kelley's official report of the action, lists 20 to 25 Confederates killed and 40 to 50 wounded while two Union soldiers were killed with three wounded and 10 missing.

Later in the day, the three citizen companies from Cumberland that had helped Kelley defend the city the day before were relieved from their active duty.

Once the city was safe, a relieved city showed its gratitude. The Cumberland City Council passed a number of resolutions to recognize Gen. Kelley and the Union Army.

The resolution read in part, "we are indebted to the brave men who risked their lives in our defence and in defence of our town and property, for the avertion of a dreadful calamity, similar to that lately inflicted upon the people of Chambersburg, by the same men who applied the torch of the incendiary to that town, and turned houseless & homeless upon the world thousands of non-combatants with their wives and children."

A parade was even help in their honor.

The near attack on the city also galvanized distaste of Confederate sympathizers in town who had been tolerated for the most part up until then.

John H. Young proposed a resolution that read, "Resolved, That all sympathizers with the rebellion, male and female, who expressed their sympathy during the late attack on our city, or who may hereafter express such sympathy, be sent by General Kelley to the so-called Southern Confederacy, where they legitimately belong."

It was "adopted with the most enthusiastic and unanimous approval," William Lowdermilk wrote in the *A History of Cumberland, Maryland.*

25

Military Justice in Cumberland

You would think that having to run into cannon fire or hack at someone with a saber would be bad enough for a man to do, but for some, it didn't seem to be enough. Those men murdered their fellow man outside of limits of the battlefield. They raped women in the towns that they invaded. They ran from the battlefield. They spied for the enemy. And many of them faced military justice because of their actions.

Records show that 267 Union soldiers were executed during the Civil War for such things as murder, rape, cowardice, desertion, mutiny, theft, pillaging and espionage. Two of the soldiers were executed in Cumberland for murdering fellow soldiers. Both court martials and executions happened in 1864.

Private Francis Gillespie of Company B of the 15th New York Cavalry Regiment was traveling with his unit on the B&O Railroad from Parkersburg, W.Va., to Cumberland. During the trip, he murdered Lieutenant William B. Shearer.

The 15th New York Cavalry had begun organizing on May 29, 1863, with Company B formed on August 8 in Syracuse. The company had left New York to begin its war service on September 2.

The *Syracuse Journal* published a letter from the officers of the 15th New York Cavalry who wrote that their unit and the army had "lost a brave, gallant and efficient officer, and that too at a time when the country most demands the exercise of such qualities as bravery, gallantry and efficiency. That this regiment in losing the benefit of his services, has sustained a loss which is nearly or quite irreparable."

The officers called Gillespie " a cowardly assassin, we can but heartily deplore."

Though Cumberland wasn't the unit's final destination (though they would return at the end of August for a two-month stay), it was for Gillespie. He was taken from the train and turned over to the Provost Marshal. No mention in the records or newspaper clippings found is a reason for the murder or how it was done. The officers' letter only mentions that Shearer died "in the immediate and vigilant discharge of his duties."

A least two military hangings took place in Cumberland during the Civil War. Courtesy of the Library of Congress.

He was court martialed on a Saturday, July 9, 1864, and hanged from a gallows near Rose Hill Cemetery on Monday, July 11 at 5 p.m.

"He ascended the scaffold with a firm step, and at the last moment said: 'I forgive everybody from the bottom of my heart and I pray God to forgive me. May the stars and stripes never be trampled on,'" wrote William Lowdermilk in *A History of Cumberland, Maryland.*

Gillespie was only 24 years old and he left behind a wife in his hometown of Syracuse, New York.

The second execution happened during the time that the 15th New York Cavalry was actually stationed in Cumberland.

On September 30, Joseph Prevost with the 1st New York Cavalry murdered Christian Miller. Following his court martial, he, too, was hanged. The members of the 15th New York were actually ordered out to witness the execution, according to *The Red Neck Ties or History of the Fifteenth New York Volunteer Cavalry*. Members of the company also acted as a guard to escort the Prevost from the prison to the gallows.

"He declared his innocence up to the last moment," Lowdermilk wrote.

"The condemned man bravely mounted the steps, the rope was adjusted, the trap sprung, when to the horror of the spectators the rope broke letting the man fall heavily to the ground. He appeared dazed at first but soon recovered and with the aid of assistants remounted the scaffold. The rope was again adjusted and he was launched into eternity," according to *The Red Neck Ties.*

The regiment had begun organizing on July 16, 1861. Nine of the companies had organized in New York City and were made up of a lot of immigrants, primarily Germans, Hungarians and Poles. One company had been organized in Philadelphia, Pa.; another in Syracuse and the last in Grand Rapids, Mich.

Though information about the murders is not found, they must have been deliberate and uncalled for. Two other soldier-on-soldier killings occurred in Cumberland in 1864, but neither of the soldiers who did the killing was executed so the instances must have been ruled accidental in those cases.

26

Teenage Rebellion, Civil War Style

Sallie Pollock rode into Cumberland on April 12, 1864, and stopped at the Revere House on Baltimore Street. The 17 years old, who one person described as a "bright, sunshiny child", went inside the hotel and met with Ira Cole. Someone she trusted had asked her to meet with the stranger to pick up a package that she would carry into the South and deliver.

Cole and Pollock met inside the hotel and Cole later testified, "I told her I wanted some confidence of her being a good Rebel and mail carrier, that this package was very important. She asked me what would convince me. I asked her if she had letters from other parties. She said one or two, then pulled out one there and showed me."

Sallie Pollock had been born in Cumberland in 1847 and had been raised on the family farm along the west bend of the Potomac River. Her mother's cousin was Captain John McNeill who led McNeill's Rangers on Confederate raids against the Union.

Sallie had been carrying packages and letters from Confederate sympathizers in Allegany County across the Potomac River since she was 14 years old. "This consisted primarily of carrying letters and information past the Union pickets and patrols along the roads and across the Potomac River to the Confederate lines," according to *Whilbr.org*.

Cole was convinced and they decided to go someplace else where he could give her the package he was carrying. They left the Revere House and headed toward the McKaig House. The McKaigs were well-known Southern sympathizers in Cumberland and Gen. David Hunter had driven some members of the family from town for a time. Another member of the family, Thomas Jefferson McKaig, had been arrested and imprisoned in Fort McHenry for his Confederate sympathies and despite the fact that he was a Maryland state senator.

"She told me that she was going to get a letter from Mrs. McKaig to make up her mail or to carry through and Mrs. McKaig would convince me that she was alright," Cole testified.

Sallie Pollock

Before they reached the McKaigs, Cole had Sallie arrested as a spy. She didn't realize that he was the cause of the arrest, though. Cole was an undercover agent who worked his way into Cumberland's Southern sympathizer community. Upon her arrest, Cole asked for all of the letters that she was carrying. The letters included notes to individual soldiers as well as letters addressed to Gen. Robert E. Lee and Confederate President Jefferson Davis.

"Dated March 24, 1864, these letters detailed the upcoming military campaign plans of General Ulysses S. Grant. Sallie had been provided this correspondence by Confederate spies and it was her job to relay the information to the Confederate lines near Cumberland," according to *Whilbr.org*.

On April 21, Sallie was tried before a military commission. The judge advocate heard the testimony and considered the evidence.

He said on May 25, 1864, "Indeed, although the accused pleads not guilty, yet after the prosecution had closed, she stated to the court that she had no testimony to offer on her behalf; although, as she has said some parts of Mr. Cole were incorrect. She further begged the commission to be as lenient as the circumstances of the case would admit, if they found her guilty."

She was found guilty and remanded to the custody of the Pennsylvania Penitentiary in Pittsburgh. This was a lenient sentence due to the petitioning of Sallie's uncle, who was a loyal Union supporter.

"After serving only seven weeks for a crime that in some cases would have resulted in death, Sallie Pollock was released from prison by order of Secretary of War, Edwin Stanton. One of the conditions of her release was that she not carry any more messages to the Confederates. Sallie went on to have two husbands and numerous children," according to *Whilbr.org*.

She died in 1890 and is buried in her family cemetery in Allegany County.

27

A Pair of Generals Give the Confederates an Ace in the Hole

During the Civil War, Cumberland, Maryland, was one of the most-well-defended cities in the Union. The city was essentially under martial law with about half of the population of 16,000 made up of Union soldiers. As a hub of transportation activity, Cumberland was important to the Union. The Baltimore and Ohio Railroad had a major stop in the city. The National Road had started in Cumberland and now ran through the city from east to west and the Chesapeake and Ohio Canal's terminus was in the city. Keeping the city safely in Union control helped keep soldiers, equipment and goods flowing quickly throughout the Union.

Yet, in this city where one out of every two people was a soldier, a small band of Confederate raiders was able to penetrate into the heart of the city and kidnap two Union brigadier generals.

The plan to kidnap Gen. Benjamin Kelley and Gen. George Crook from Cumberland did not originate with Lt. Jesse McNeill. It was an idea his father had had but never been able to execute. His father, Capt. John McNeill, was the original commander of the notorious McNeill's Rangers.

Capt. McNeill organized his men as Partisan Rangers under the authority of the Confederate Congress. They cooperated with the Confederate Army but operated independently.[23] Capt. McNeill had 210 men under his command, though no more than two-thirds were ever together at once.[24] Capt. McNeill and his men ranged throughout the Potomac Valley raiding Union outposts and supply trains and disrupting operations of the Union Army. They were effective at their work.

The rangers attacked a Union supply train of eighty wagons nearly Burlington, WV, on November 16, 1863. The rebels captured twenty men and 245 horses and set the wagons on fire.

"Captain McNeill took to the mountains, and by a wonderful march (for rapidity) escaped, though pursued by over six hundred men," Confederate General John Imboden wrote of the incident.[25] McNeill lost only one man and had five wounded.

In 1864, the Rangers captured Romney, WV, and held it for three days.[26]

"One expedition after another was sent out by General Kelley, the Union commander in his front, for the purpose of crushing him; and in giving orders to his subordinate officers the injunction was invariably repeated to 'Kill, capture, or drive McNeill out of the country!'" Ranger John Fay wrote about life with Capt. McNeill.[27]

Capt. McNeill's daring-do ended in October 1864. Confederate General Jubal Early's men were retreating in the face of General Philip Sheridan's Union forces. Though Sheridan was in Harrisonburg, VA, the supply train supplying his men stretched back toward the north. Near Mt. Jackson, VA, the wagons crossed a bridge over the Shenandoah River that guarded by a hundred Union soldiers.

Sixty of McNeill's Rangers attacked the supply train and soldiers at dawn on October 2, 1864, hoping to provide some relief to General Early. Capt. McNeill rode into the battle screaming the rebel yell. At one point in the battle, he fell from a wound through the shoulder that lodged in the base of his spine.

Lt. Jesse McNeill rode to his father's side and Capt. McNeill told him, "take command and show yourself a man."[28] Capt. McNeill told his men to leave him because he was too wounded, but Jesse refused to leave him. Instead Jesse McNeill and the Rangers took Capt. McNeill to the home of Rev. Addison Weller, a Methodist minister who lived nearby. Weller's wife, Elizabeth, wrote later:

> "We saw at a glance he was severely wounded, as they filed into the yard, and lifted him from his faithful old horse and laid him on the grass. His noble form, writhing in agony, reminded one more of a wounded lion. The fire still flashed form his clear blue eyes. . . . As his men bent over him with tears of sympathy, he looked into their faces and said:

'Goodbye, my boys, leave me to my fate, I can do no more for my country.' One of his men knelt and offered up a short prayer, commending their gallant leader to a merciful God. As he arose and left with the men, the Captain's eyes followed them as long as they were in sight. Then for the first time, he exclaimed: 'Oh, I am in such agony; do something for me if you can!'[29"]

Union General Benjamin Kelley

Mrs. Weller was unable to treat the wound because she could not remove the bullet in Capt. McNeill's spine. So she tried to ease his pain and she cut his beard to disguise him from Union forces that began searching for the famed Ranger when they heard he had been wounded.[30]

Meanwhile, Jesse rode fifty miles to fetch his mother and bring her back to her husband. The Union soldiers eventually discovered him, but they also realized that he was too sick to be moved.

However, wily to the last, the Rangers snuck in, carried Capt. McNeill to a carriage and took him south to Harrisonburg. McNeill lingered near death for two more weeks before he died on November 10, 1864, in the arms of his wife and surrounded by friends.[31]

Planning the raid

Lt. Jesse McNeill had something to prove. He had lived in his father's shadow all of his life. McNeill decided that if he could pull off a feat that his father hadn't been able to do, then it would prove that the son was the rightful successor to his father's command of the Rangers. McNeill also wanted to do it for the same reason his father had. In 1863, Kelley had arrested McNeill's mother, sister and four-year-old nephew.[32] The group escaped shortly after their arrest and made their way to Capt. John McNeill's headquarters in Moorefield, W.Va. When Capt. McNeill heard was had happened, he said, "General Kelley will regret that, for I will go into Cumberland and kidnap him and carry him off."[33]

What's more is that Jesse McNeill and Kelley were interested in the same woman. Mary Clara Bruce lived in Cumberland and McNeill had courted her before the war. Once the fighting between the Union and Confederacy began and McNeill had to stay away from the city, word reached him that Kelley had started courting the young woman.[34]

Soon after McNeill took command of the Rangers, he was forced into bed rest for weeks when he broke his ankle in December 1864. During that time, he had plenty of time to think and develop his revenge against Kelley.[35]

For McNeill and his Rangers to get to Kelley, they would need knowledge of the Union's defense of Cumberland. John Lynn, Jr., one of the Rangers, was a native of the city. McNeill granted him a furlough to return home and perform reconnaissance of the town. However, Lynn was captured on February 5, 1865, and imprisoned at Fort McHenry in Baltimore. He was listed as a "Guerrilla-not to be exchanged during the war."[36]

Obtaining good intelligence was so critical to the mission that McNeill sent Sgt. John Fay, another Cumberlander to scout out the city. Fay entered the city twice to collect information about the Union defenses and where Kelley stayed. Friends and Confederate sympathizers "obtained thorough information as to the number of troops in Cumberland, the location of the various headquarters" and where Union pickets were stationed.[37]

Union General George Crook

On February 19, Fay sent Pvt. Cephas Hallar who had accompanied him to Cumberland back to meet with McNeill and deliver the information that had been collected.

Once he knew what he faced, McNeill gathered an incursion force that included forty-eight of his own men and fifteen men from

Company F, 7th Virginia Cavalry and Company D, 11th Virginia Cavalry. Jesse told them of the danger of the mission and said he only wanted volunteers to go. If anyone wanted to back out, he could remove himself without shame. None did. [38]The men and their mounts were equipped and ready to go. They set out for Cumberland on the 20th of February 1865 crossing small ridges and creeks until they reached Knobley Mountain near the Potomac River in Mineral County, West Virginia. The snow drifts on the mountain were deep and slowed them down and they had to dismount and clear a path for themselves and their horses. Once over the mountain, they crossed the river at the Samuel Brady Farm.

Kidnapped!

George Stanton met them near the Samuel Brady Farm and told the Confederate Rangers that the everything was still quiet in Cumberland, though he had seen Union cavalry pass through on their way to New Creek, W.Va.[39] He also informed the group that not only was Kelley in town but so was Gen. Crook.[40] Now the attractiveness of the mission was irresistible. The mission to kidnap one general now became a mission to kidnap two.

The Rangers were now five miles away from Cumberland along the New Creek road, a well guarded route. Fay's plan had the rebels riding around Cresaptown to reach the National Road and coming into Cumberland from the northwest through the Narrows, the gap in Will's Mountain that the National Road ran through. It was not guarded with pickets, but it was also twice as long a route, which might mean it would be daybreak before they reached Cumberland. That meant more of a risk of being seen and an alarm sounded.

McNeill called a war council and laid out the options to the Rangers: give up the mission, use the New Creek Road and risk being stopped by the pickets or raid the pickets at the railroad station near Brady's Mills.[41] The Rangers unanimously decided on the latter and to continue on for the big prize of two major generals.

McNeill and Sgt. Joseph Vandiver led the Rangers north on New Creek Road toward Cumberland. The cold of the night had combined with the snow on the ground to form a crust that cracked under the horses' hooves creating more sound than the group would have liked. They traveled two miles before they came upon the first picket.

"Halt! Who comes there?" the sentry called.
"Friends from New Creek," McNeill replied.
"Dismount one, come forward and give the countersign."

Instead, McNeill put the spurs to his horse. It jumped forward. As McNeill passed the sentry, he fired his pistol in the man's face. Though not injured, the man was shaken.

Two other soldiers with the sentry had been sitting under a shelter trying to warm themselves around a fire. Hearing they commotion, they headed toward the river, but were quickly caught.[42]

When the captured soldiers weren't willing to give up the countersign, McNeill threatened to kill them. They still refused so McNeill put his pistol to one man's forehead and prepared to fire. The men still said nothing. One of the Rangers suggested hanging the man to choke the countersign from him. A halter was placed around the man's neck and the soldier quickly told the Rangers what the countersign was.[43]

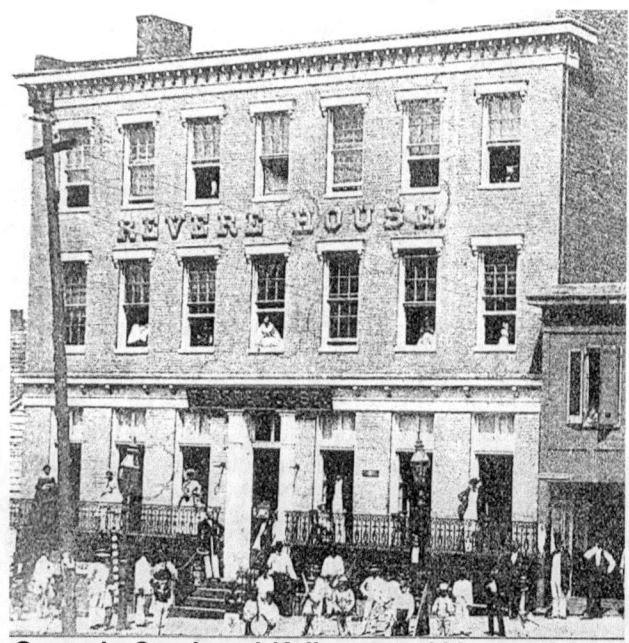

Generals Crook and Kelley were kidnapped from the Revere House during the Civil War. Courtesy of *Whilbr.org*.

The men were then taken as prisoners along with the Rangers so that they wouldn't give away the Confederates' mission.

Another mile along the road brought the Rangers to the next picket. The countersign "Bull's Gap" was given and the Rangers approached. Once they reached the sentry, they moved swiftly to capture the guard and keep him from issuing a warning. Not only did they capture the guard, but the Rangers captured five other soldiers who were playing cards around the warmth of a fire. The Rangers broke the soldiers muskets and told them to remain where they were until morning when they would be paroled.

By 3 a.m., the McNeill's Rangers approached downtown Cumberland from the west. They rode their horses down Greene Street, crossed the iron bridge over Will's Creek and continued down Baltimore Street toward the Barnum House and Revere House, the hotels where Kelley and Crook were staying. The men whistled tunes and exchanged greetings with any soldiers or people they met in the dim light of pre-dawn. Some of the men had even put on the blue army coats from the captured pickets.[44]

At the Barnum House, the Rangers separated into four groups. One group went to the stables to gather the horses there. Fay led another group to the telegraph office to destroy the equipment and cut the lines. These actions would delay any pursuit or notification of Union forces to the south, giving the Rangers time to get safety. They didn't do a thorough job, though, and the damage was repaired soon after the Rangers left Cumberland.[45]

Each hotel had a sentry in front of it, but neither soldier was concerned at the sight of the men. Why should they be? They were in the heart of a city that had 8,000 soldiers in it. Sprigg Lynn, a Ranger from Cumberland, dismounted. He captured and disarmed the sentry in front of the Barnum House without the alarm being raised. He learned which room was Kelley's and then he, Joseph Kuykendall, John Cunningham and John Daily entered the building. The Rangers found Kelley asleep in his room on the second floor. They roused him and told him he was a prisoner.[46] His adjutant, Maj. Thayer Melvin, was also arrested. The men were allowed to dress and then led outside.[47]

The group sent to kidnap Crook[48] ran into a problem. Though the general was asleep, a sentinel challenged the group at the entrance.

He was quickly overpowered, but then the Rangers discovered the door to the Revere House was locked. One of the men knocked on the door. A black servant answered. When the soldiers ordered him to take them to Gen. Crook, the young man complied. The Rangers entered the hotel.[49]

"While Vandiver and Dailey were getting a light in the office below, Gassman went to No. 46, General Crook's apartment, and thinking the door was locked, knocked at it several times. A voice within asked: 'Who's there?' Gassman replied: 'A friend,' and was told to come in. Vandiver, Tucker, and Dailey arrived by this time and all four entered the room. Approaching the bed where the General lay, Vandiver said in a pompous manner, 'General Crook, you are my prisoner.' 'What authority have you for this?' inquired the general. 'The authority of General Rosser, of Fitzhugh Lee's division of cavalry,' said Vandiver in response. Crook then rose up in bed and asked: 'Is General Rosser here?' 'Yes,' replied Vandiver, 'I am General Rosser. We have surprised and captured the town.' That settled the matter as far as the bona fide general was concerned. He was immensely surprised at the bold announcement, but knowing nothing to the contrary, accepted Vandiver's assertion as the truth. He submitted to his fate with as much grace and cheerfulness as he could muster."[50]

The kidnappings were carried out so quietly that other guests and officers, "who were sleeping in adjoining rooms were not disturbed."[51]

When the Rangers walked out of the hotel, a clerk came out behind them and asked how many Confederates they had captured. By the time he realized he had made a mistake, John Taylor grabbed the clerk's hat, John Cunningham rifled the man's pockets and W. H. Maloney jerked the clerk's overcoat over his head. The Rangers left motionless and dumbfounded on the sidewalk.[52]

Twenty five minutes after entering the city, the Rangers were leaving with their generals.[53] While kidnapping two generals was a major coup for the Rangers, they might also have captured two future United States Presidents had they tried to kidnap all of the officers in the hotels. Brigadier General Rutherford B. Hayes and Major William McKinley were both sleeping in the Barnum House.[54] "Brigadier Generals Lightburn and Duvall were also temporarily sojourning there; but we were not then aware of the fact, or a greater supply of Generals might have been secured," Fay wrote later.[55]

On the way out of the town, the Rangers stopped once more to take a number of horses from the government stable so that they would have spare mounts. They encountered little resistance on the way out of the city. A dozen pickets were captured near the C&O Canal. Their weapons were destroyed and they were left behind.

Another group of pickets was encountered a short distance further on. One of the sentries asked, "Sergeant, shall I fire?"

Vandiver, acting angry, shouted, "If you do, I will place you under arrest. This is General Crook's bodyguard, and we have no time to waste. The rebels are coming, and we are going out to meet them."

The sentries were fooled and allowed to pass.[56]

The Rangers were four or five miles from Cumberland when they heard the boom of a cannon that told them their kidnapping had been discovered and the alarm was being raised. "The alarm was given within ten minutes by a negro watchman at the hotel who escaped from them, and within an hour we had a party of fifty cavalry after them," [57]Maj. Robert Kennedy, wrote to Union General Phillip Sheridan who was in Winchester, Virginia, at the time.

Ransomed in Richmond

Though the men were away from Cumberland, they rode with a chance that Union troops throughout the area might be encountered. The Rangers only began to feel safe when they reached Moorefield, West Virginia, having traveled 90 miles in a 24 hour period.

The generals were treated well during their capture. The Rangers took the generals to Staunton, Virginia, and then to Richmond where they were imprisoned in Libby Prison.[58] Before taking his leave of the generals, McNeill even gave them a pint of whiskey and $65 to show he had no hard feelings toward them.[59]

Though it was expected that the generals would be returned to the Union, McNeill hoped to have them exchanged for some of his men imprisoned at Fort McHenry in Baltimore.[60] The generals were eventually exchanged on Mar. 20, 1864 for Brig. Gen. Isaac Trimble who had been wounded and captured at the Battle of Gettysburg.

The boldness of the kidnapping gave the Confederacy encouragement when there were little to be found near the end of the war.

Years later, Virginia Gov. Charles O'Ferrall called the kidnapping, "as bold and successful achievement as any during the war, and deserves a place in every book which treats of that stormy period."[61]

Captain William N. McDonald wrote that "The capture of two distinguished Federal Generals Crook and Kelley . . . was an event that excited the North with astonishment at the audacity, and the South with admiration for its boldness and exultation over its success."[62]

28

In the Wake of Assassination

Cumberland seemed unusually quiet on April 15, 1865. Though residents walked the streets, they spoke quietly to each other. "On every face could be plainly traced sorrow, sadness, gloom or indignation," reported *The Alleganian* newspaper.

Rumor was spreading quickly through the city, but it wasn't until around noon that an official telegram making the rumor true.

President Abraham Lincoln had been assassinated.

The president had attended a showing of *Our American Cousin* at Ford's Theater on Good Friday, April 14. John Wilkes Booth, seeking to strike a blow for the defeated Confederate States of America, shot Lincoln in the back of the head. Booth had escaped capture and the president had been carried across the street to a private boarding house. He died there on Saturday morning at 7:22 a.m. without ever regaining consciousness.

"When the truth was made known, all business was suspended, and by request of the Mayor, all the Church and fire-alarm bells of the city were tolled for one hour," *The Alleganian* reported.

On Monday afternoon, Mayor C. H. Ohr called a special meeting at the courthouse "to give expression to our feelings on this sad occassion." Officers were appointed and a committee formed on the spot to draft a resolution, which was approved by the entire group.

The resolution read, in part: "Resolved, That though our lamented President was not permitted by Divine Providence to enter upon the full realization of all his hopes and wishes, yet he lived long enough to be rejoiced at the near approach to, and successful result of the many cares and anxieties through which he had passed in his untiring efforts to restore peace and union and kind feelings to every part of this Nation.

"Resolved, That we have no words with which we can adequately express the deep horror and detestation that we feel for the foul deed which has deprived this good man of his life, and bowed down with sadness and sorrow the heart of this great Nation."

The committee also agreed that during the president's funeral, all businesses in the city would be closed and the bells of the churches would toll.

The group also created a committee of 11 to decide upon any further observances on the passing of the president.

Lincoln's funeral was held in Washington, D.C. on Wednesday, April 19. The body lay in state in the East Room of the White House until 9 a.m. when a solemn procession began through the city to the U.S. Capitol. At the Capitol, 600 dignitaries who had received tickets to the service began arriving around 10 a.m. The service began at noon. Four different clergymen officiated over the service.

In Cumberland, the city observed the president's funeral as agreed upon. "In many places, the national colors, draped in black, were displayed at half-mast, and the gloom was universal. A pall of blackness seemed to enshroud the popular heart, and a general feeling of sorrow, grief and horror at the terrible and unparalleled tragedy that had called forth these outward manifestations—this sable garniture of woe was unmistakably portrayed in the countenances of our people.—At morning, noon and night, the church and fire bells were tolled, and services appropriate to the solemn occasion were held in the churches of the various denominations. At noon a salute of twenty-one minute guns were fired and continued at intervals of half an hour during the afternoon, the observance of the day closing with a national salute at sunset," reported *The Alleganian*.

29

Both Armies Wanted Romney, Neither Could Hold It

To live in Romney during the Civil War was to wonder each morning which state and even which country you lived in. Virginia or West Virginia? The United States of America or the Confederate States of America?

It's not that the 450 residents were confused. They considered themselves Virginians in the Confederate States of America. However, what they believed mattered little when political shenanigans or military might were involved.

"Romney switched hands a lot of times, but a lot of that is simply counting when an army passed through town, which is a lot different than occupying it," said Romney local historian Royce Saville.

The oft-quoted number for how many times Romney changed from Union control to Confederate control or vice versa using the loose standard is 56 times. That still only puts that town in second place for the most-traded town in the war. Winchester, VA, is said to have switched hands 72 times during the war. Even under stricter standards for what constitutes control, Romney's switches remain in the double digits.

"Romney was on the transportation route south from Cumberland (MD) and west," said Romney Mayor Daniel Hileman. "The troops and supplies would come in on the railroad and then come south through Romney."

The railroad represented one of the Union's main supply lines to troops serving in Ohio and points west. Romney became the base of operations for many Confederate attacks against the railroad or the Chesapeake and Ohio Canal. The town was strongly Southern in its support and it was close to both the railroad and canal and it was located on good roads that allowed for quick troop movements.

Gen. Kelley's men crossing the wire bridge at Romney. Courtesy of *Harper's Weekly*.

Still Virginia

When the Civil War broke out with the bombardment of Fort Sumter, Romney and Hampshire County were still part of Virginia. The men in Romney enlisted in Virginia army units and went off to fight for Virginia and the Confederacy. By the war's end, 13 companies of Confederate soldiers would be formed in Hampshire County while only one Union company would be raised. Hu Maxwell and H.L. Swisher estimate in *History of Hampshire County, West Virginia* estimate that around 1,200 Hampshire County men or half of the county men joined the Confederate Army.

Virginia seceded from the Union on April 17, 1861, and less than two months later, Romney changed hands for the first time. Col. Lew Wallace and the 11th Indiana Zouaves came through the Mechanicsburg Gap headed toward Romney.

"On coming within a mile of Romney we were fired on by the picket-guard of the rebels, while passing through a defile walled in by tremendous cliffs. At the sound of the first gun, however, we deployed as skirmishers, and being scattered thus no one was hurt on our side. We returned their fire and killed one of the picket. He was seen to fall and slide down the side of the mountain about twenty feet, when his body lodged against a tree," wrote James Gookins, an embedded reporter with the Union Army writing for *Harper's Weekly*.

The Confederate forces were on the other side of the bridge that led into the town. They had cannon trained on the passage across it.

"[O]ur men, however, dashed forward through the bridge with a yell, when the cowards (of whom there was quite a large body posted on the hills) fled without firing a shot from their cannon," Gookins wrote.

One of the battles for Romney during the Civil War. Courtesy of *Harper's Weekly*.

When the Zouaves took the bridge, they were fired on from Confederates hidden in a nearby house. The Zouaves charged the house firing as they fled and the remaining Confederate soldiers retreated. The 400 Confederate soldiers retreated so quickly that they left behind "baggage, some rifles, tents, swords, pistols, etc., etc. We took seven officers' marquees, a quantity of uniforms, and large quantities of clothing, a secession flag, four horses (one of which was the rebel colonel's riding-horse), four large chests of ammunition, camp equipage, and a great variety of other articles," according to Gookins. The bounty filled three wagons.

Wallace and the Zouaves occupied the town for a few hours on June 13, mainly as they collected what had been left behind. The fighting left two Confederate soldiers dead and a couple men on both sides wounded.

By the next day, Confederate forces commanded by Col. A.P. Hill would occupy the town. Much of the changes in control were similarly bloodless with one group waiting until the town was empty before occupying it.

This is not to say that there wasn't any fighting. On Sept. 23, 1861, Confederate Col. Angus McDonald and his men of the 114th and 77th Virginia militia were occupying Romney when it was attacked by the Union army, consisting of the 4th and 8th Ohio and some of Ringgold's cavalry, that attacked from Hanging Rock to the north. McDonald was forced to retreat in the face of a larger army on the 24th, but he retook the town on the 25th and the Union army retreated to New Creek, VA (now Keyser, WV).

Disrupting the Town

Once war broke out, part of Hampshire County's population was made up of soldiers. Sometimes they were Confederate, sometimes Union and sometimes both.

"The county was never free from soldiers from the day the ordinance of secession was passed by the Richmond convention until peace was restored," according to Maxwell and Swisher.

For the most part, fighting took place outside of the town limits and residents kept their heads indoors and out of the way of bullets. Better to just let an army pass through than to attract gunfire into your home by saying or doing the wrong thing. In January 1862, the Union army captured Romney and occupied the town for most of the month.

"When they left, they ransacked the court house and threw the land books and court records into the street," Saville said.

Some of the books were destroyed and others were lost forever. With no records, legal transactions were pretty much shut down. Some of the books were later found in North Carolina and returned to the town. This did not endear the Union Army to the resident, but Romney fared better than Frenchburg.

"It was a thriving town nearly as big as Romney," Saville said. "The Union laid waste to it so that it never recovered."

Some buildings in Romney were burned but the town survived and recovered.

The Romney Court House. Courtesy of Wikimedia Commons.

A New State

Many of the westernmost counties in Virginia depended on the B&O Railroad for their economic health so when Virginia seceded, local leaders and Union officials began making plans that lead to the creation of a new state. As a coalition of counties was formed to secede from Virginia, Hampshire found itself part of the coalition, though it, and Romney, which was the county seat, identified more with the Confederates.

"Romney was absolutely Confederate," Saville said. "The railroad is the reason that Hampshire, Morgan, Berkeley and Jefferson counties are in West Virginia. They needed to be in the Union."

He points out that when the vote to break away from Virginia came, there were less than 2,000 eligible votes in Hampshire County and less than 160 voted.

"Most of those who voted were known Union soldiers or union in their sympathies," Saville said. "Only nine voted note to go, but many who would have voted that way were off fighting."

West Virginia was formed on June 20, 1863. This did not stop the town from being passed back and forth. Besides the Union and Confederate armies holding Romney, Confederate guerillas, specifically McNeill's Rangers, occupy the town from time to time.

The Confederate veterans memorial at Romney. Courtesy of Wikimedia Commons.

A Union State

Things did not improve in Romney in the Union. In fact, they were worse. Not only did the back and forth occupation continue, but Romney saw much of its autonomy vanish. The occupying army command made many decisions for the town. A Union-appointed sheriff enforced and the laws and later in the war, the county capital was moved from Romney to Piedmont because Piedmont supported the Union.

The Union Army also took steps to rout out Confederate sympathizers along its supply line into the Shenandoah Valley.

"The Union practically burned everything within a 15 mile path from Hanging Rock to Romney," Saville said.

Aftermath

When the war ended, the bitterness did not. Soldiers returned to find their homes and farms devastated and their state gone. They were now in a new state and were not allowed to vote because they had fought on the losing side of the war.

The western portion of Hampshire County, which had been more Union in its sympathies, broke off and formed Mineral County in 1866.

In 1867, the town erected the first monument to Confederate soldiers.

"It was to honor the Confederate soldiers who came back to nothing in a state that hadn't existed when they left," Saville said.

Many residents refused to write West Virginia as their state. They continued writing Romney, Virginia. When the ex-Confederates got their voting rights back in 1872 they quickly elected the state's first Democrat governor.

Now, 150 years later, Hileman said Romney will be holding events to remember the Civil War throughout the sesquicentennial with the largest ones being planned for 2013.

For more information on Romney in the Civil war, visit: Historic Hampshire County, West Virginia (*www.historichampshire.org*).

30

Reburying the Dead

They gave the "last full measure" in their service to their country, whether it was the United States or Confederate States of America, but when they died, it was in Allegany County where they were buried. One third of the states in both the Union and Confederacy had dead buried in the county at the end of the Civil War.

Many of these men had died far from their homes and families, but rather than have their bodies returned to their families they were buried in various cemeteries around the county. The reason was simple. With embalming still not commonly used, there was no way to ship the bodies the distances required in some cases without them starting to decay. Then there was the problem that many of the soldiers served in the Confederacy, which was not exactly welcoming of trains from the North.

After hostilities ended, however, many families from the South came searching for their sons and husbands who never returned home. Those that were found in Allegany County were disinterred and finally sent home with their families.

A more-ambitious movement of military bodies started in 1866, though. The federal government had established the Antietam National Cemetery in Washington County in 1865 for the war dead from the battle at Antietam. By 1866, the scope of the cemetery had expanded to include any unclaimed war dead in Western Maryland "believing that course to be in accordance with the patriotic spirit with which the appropriations were made for the establishment of the Cemetery," according to the book, *History of Antietam National Cemetery.*

As each body was located and disinterred, the body was placed in a coffin and transported to the cemetery superintendent who oversaw the reburial. Every coffin was numbered and then that number was recorded in a book along with the soldier's name, company, regiment and state when all of the information was available. The graves were laid out in such a way "that a person occupying a position in the center of the grounds, with his face turned to any point of the compass, can, with a good field glass, read the inscription on every head-board contained therein," according to *History of Antietam National Cemetery*.

Graves of the soldiers who fell at Antietam. Courtesy of the Library of Congress.

The United States Burial Corps began the process of exhuming and reburying bodies in October 1866 and continued until January 1867 when bad weather brought it to a halt. It recommenced in April and finished in September. It was a massive undertaking not only in Allegany County, but also Frederick and Washington counties.

The cemetery initially held 4,667 bodies from 34 locations in Maryland. The 389 bodies removed from Allegany County came from Cumberland, Clarysville, Oldtown, Frostburg, Little Orleans and Westernport.

The fallen soldiers in Allegany County came from 12 of the 36 states and territories in the U.S. in 1865. They were: West Virginia (98), Ohio (95), Pennsylvania (35), Indiana (28), New York (25), Illinois (10), Massachusetts (10), Michigan (10), Maryland (5), New Jersey (3), Connecticut (1) and Vermont (1). There were also six men who were U.S. Regulars and 62 whose home state was unknown.

Though the county also had Confederate dead, these bodies were not exhumed for reburial at Antietam. Some of them remain buried in Allegany County even today. Only Union soldiers are buried in Antietam National Cemetery. This is because of the bitterness that still existed between the North and the South over the Civil War. Confederate bodies were re-interred in Washington Confederate Cemetery in Hagerstown, Mt. Olivet Cemetery in Frederick and Elmwood Cemetery in Shepherdstown, WV. According to the National Park Service, about 2,800 Confederate soldiers are buried in these cemeteries and 60 percent are unidentified.

Antietam National Cemetery was dedicated on September 17, 1867, the fifth anniversary of the Battle of Antietam. President Andrew Johnson said during the ceremony, "When we look on yon battlefield, I think of the brave men who fell in the fierce struggle of battle, and who sleep silent in their graves. Yes, many of them sleep in silence and peace within this beautiful enclosure after the earnest conflict has ceased."

31

Honoring Those Who Served in the Civil War

Once the Civil War had ended and the lives of Western Maryland residents got back to normal, they began to honor their veterans of the war ... all of their veterans. In some states residents paid homage to either their Confederate veterans or Union veterans. Though Maryland had been a Union state, it had a significant number of veterans who fought on both sides of the war.

Union Monument

Allegany County's first Civil War veteran's monument to honor Union soldiers was erected in 1895, 30 years after the end of the war.

The monument stands in Rose Hill Cemetery in Cumberland and features a soldier standing atop a stone pedestal. "The solitary common soldier statue was the most popular monument form after the Civil War in recognition of the loss of 600,000 men; it symbolized the democratic ideal of the individual," according to the Maryland Military Monument Commission.

Besides the unveiling of the monument, events of the day included decorating the veterans' graves in the county with flowers and a parade that ran from the G.A.R. Hall on Baltimore Street to Rose Hill Ceremony for the monument unveiling. An estimated 5,000 people attended the ceremony at Rose Hill Cemetery.

"The graves upon which we lay flowers today contains all that is mortal of our noble soldier dead, and as they were true to their country while living, let each succeeding generation keep their memory green while dead," Col. G.W.F. Vernon of Baltimore said during his address at the unveiling ceremony.

"Rose Hill cemetery never looked lovelier than it did today," the

Cumberland Evening Times reported. "It was so warm that under every shade tree groups of people were seeking shelter."

The Cumberland Women's Relief Corps erected the bronze monument "with contributions of citizens, to honor the men of our county, who fought for the Union 1861-1865," according to the monument's plaque. The American Bronze Company in Chicago, Ill., cast the statue.

The Women's Relief Corps was part of the Ladies Auxiliary of the Tyler Post of the Grand Army of the Republic. The members of the Cumberland Women's Relief Corps included: President Amanda C. Schmutz, Chairwoman Barbara Schilling, Susan B. Shuck, Louisa J. Smith, Annie Warnick, Lizzie B. Keller, Mary A. Kitzmiller and Belle F. Davis.

The monument was dedicated on Memorial Day, May 30, 1895, during a sunny, pleasant summer day. "While the people of this glorious nation were mourning their honored dead all heaven seemed to smile upon them with a smile of sympathy," the *Cumberland Evening Times* reported.

The Maryland Military Monuments Commission cleaned and waxed the bronze monument in 1997 and has routinely performed maintenance on it.

Confederate Monument

It took another 17 years before the county was ready to honor its Confederate soldiers with a monument. "Although erected almost fifty years after the close of the Civil War, Cumberland was still one of the first cities in Maryland to erect a monument in honor of the Confederate dead," Al Feldstein wrote in *Feldstein's Gone But Not Forgotten, Volume II.*

The monument, which was also located in the Rose Hill Cemetery, was dedicated in 1912 "to the heroes who died fighting for the lost cause." The monument also marks the burial site of six Confederate soldiers who died at the Clarysville Hospital while they were POW's there. Those soldiers were:
- Allen Brown, Co. C of the 57th Regiment North Carolina (died October 11, 1864)
- H.W. Fullenwider, 2nd Lieutenant, Co. E, 23rd Regiment North Carolina (died July 29, 1864)
- N. H. Gilbert, Sergeant, Co. F, 58th Regiment Virginia (died

August 9, 1864)
- Watson M. Ramsey, Co. F, 58th Regiment Virginia (died August 7, 1864)
- John A. Smith, Co. E, 52nd Regiment Virginia (died August 1, 1864)
- Joel R. Stow, Co. A, 8th Tennessee Cavalry (died April 8, 1865)

Western Maryland's Historical Library also notes that three other Confederate soldiers (one unknown and two who died at the Battle of Folck's Mill) were interred at the Confederate monument. "The burial vault was prepared under the auspices of James Breathed Camp of the United Confederate Veterans," according to the library's web site.

The monument cost $500 and the Daughters of the Confederacy raised funds to improve the grounds around the monument, which was dedicated on June 11, 1912. The keynote speaker was Robert E. Lee, Jr. "The address of Mr. Lee was couched in beautiful language and in keeping with that oratory for which the southland is noted," the Cumberland Evening Times reported.

U.S. Colored Troops Monument

The Cumberland Historic Cemetery Association dedicated one final monument to county residents who fought in the Civil War on May 27, 1991. This monument honored U.S. Colored Troop, six of whom are buried in Sumner Cemetery. The cemetery on Yale Street in Cumberland is the oldest black cemetery in the county.

The six soldiers served in the 30th Regiment Infantry of the U.S. Colored Troops, which was formed in Maryland in February 1864. The Allegany County soldiers were:
- Francis "Frank" Taylor
- Thomas Lindsey
- Abraham Craig
- Thomas Simpson
- Sam Parry
- Hannibal Kinner

32

How Antietam Was Remembered 50 Years Later

As Western Maryland prepares to remember the 150th anniversary of the Battle of Antietam in Sharpsburg, no actual Civil War veterans will be attending. The last major anniversary event for a Civil War battle that saw actual veterans in attendance was the 75th anniversaries. Antietam's 75th anniversary was in 1937.

For Washington County residents, the event also represented the bicentennial of the settling of the county and the 175th anniversary of the founding of Hagerstown. The latter events had been originally planned for 1935, but they had been postponed because of the country's poor economic condition. The money just wasn't there to plan for a big event.

However, remembering Antietam was not only a big event, but it was a federal one. President Franklin Roosevelt created the National Antietam Commemoration Commission and appointed Maryland U.S. Senator Millard Tydings to chair it, along with members Maryland U.S. Senator George Radcliffe, Congressman David Lewis and General Milton Reckord of Maryland, Virginia U.S. Senator Henry Byrd and Vermont Congressman Charles Plumley. Maryland Governor Harry Nice of Maryland appointed a Maryland State Advisory Committee. Park Loy was the Secretary and Treasurer of the Commission and the Chair of the Washington County Historical Society, which was responsible for much of the organization of the events.

As the anniversary date approached, estimates were that a quarter million people, including President Roosevelt, would be attending the event.

Events were planned over two weeks from September 4 to 17. Some days were themed like "National Anthem Day", "Baltimore

City Day" and "Defenders' Day." At times, the events seemed more appropriate to a county with livestock shows and a carnival midway.

The souvenir guide from the 75th anniversary of the Battle of Antietam. It focused on the peace between the North and the South. Courtesy of *Whilbr.org*.

Maryland Motorist Magazine described the events this way: "For two weeks it will feature a 'junior world's fair' complete with large-scale historical pageant and, on its final and climatic day, will mark the 75th anniversary of the Battle of Antietam by re-enacting that famous struggle on the battlefield—following an address expected to be delivered by President Roosevelt. ... The visitor will find many attractions for his attention. A gala carnival midway, a stately museum overflowing with objects of rare historical interest, a series of villages depicting life in foreign countries, a glorious field of flowers on the approach to the Horticultural Hall, a long Industrial Court displaying some of the earliest curiosities and some of the latest wonders in manufacturing, a Travel Building devoted to the visual store of ancient and modern transportation, the Paradise Gardens where all the animals and all the plants will flourish, a Commercial Building where hundreds of nation wide wholesalers and retailers will spread their wares before the world, and finally the great dramatic spectacle 'On Wings of Time.'"

Twenty-one governors of the 29 of the states whose troops fought the Battle of Antietam attended the climatic day that featured the re-enactment, along with President Roosevelt. National Guardsmen of Maryland, Pennsylvania and Virginia re-enacted the "Bloody Lane" phase of the battle. About 1,500 men took part in the re-enactment will be 900 of them in the Union army and 600 in the Southern army.

President Roosevelt spoke to the gathered crowd across from the Dunkard Church where part of the battle occurred. Sharpsburg citizens presented him with a section of a tree hewn on the battlefield that contained a bullet fired during the battle. Roosevelt told the audience, "In the presence of the spirits of those who fell on this field - Union soldiers and Confederate soldiers - we can believe that they rejoice with us in the unity of understanding which is so increasingly ours today. They urge us on in all we do to foster that unity in the spirit of tolerance, of willingness to help our neighbor, and of faith in the destiny of the United States."

About 50 Civil War veterans attended the events; most of them in their 90's. Though there were a few thousand Civil War veterans still alive in 1937, less than 100 actually fought at Antietam.

The bitterness of 75 years prior had disappeared and "frequently men who fought for the South were seen arm in arm with soldiers of the North," according to the *Hagerstown Morning Herald*. In one memorable picture, Cpl. Bazel Lemley, 94, of the Confederate Army, shook hands with Gen. Benjamin Franklin Red of the Union Army at Bloody Lane where they had tried to kill each other in 1862.

President Franklin D. Roosevelt at the 75th Anniversary of the Battle of Antietam. Courtesy of Whilbr.org.

33

Who is "Genl. Scofield"?

As the country remembers the men who fought in the Civil War 150 years ago, a general lies forgotten in a grave atop Meadow Mountain just off of old U.S. Route 40. The only clue to who this man was is a grave marker that answers few questions and raises more.

IN MEMORY OF
GENL. SCOFIELD
CIVIL WAR VETERAN
KILLED ON THIS MOUNTAIN
1894
Donated by
A.J. IRWIN & SON

For years, Marie Lancaster of Addison, Pa., cared for the grave making sure the grave was trimmed and occasionally bringing flowers or a U.S. flag to leave by the marker.

"We just saw the grave while we were taking a Sunday drive and, after looking at it up close, my husband and I were of the opinion that a high-ranking military man like Gen. Scofield deserved a more prominent burial place than an isolated spot on the side of a mountain," Lancaster said in a 1992 interview with the *Cumberland Sunday Times*.

The tombstone notes that the general was "killed" rather than died. The Frostburg Museum has some recollections from Arthur Irwin who is the son in A.J. Irwin and Son. The Irwin family operated a monument business on Main Street in Frostburg for many decades.

James Rada, Jr.

The interviewer wrote, "About the time of the Civil War, an officer on his way back from Washington DC with his mustering out pay was murdered and buried on Meadow Mountain. Sometime later, Red's father made a copy of the inscription made on a wooden grave marker. He then made a stone monument for the grave which can be seen as you ride by on Route 40."

Searching through newspapers available from 1894, no mention of a murder of a veteran or a general.

The man buried in the grave is not any known General Scofield. Research through Civil War veteran databases and pension records shows only two Civil War generals with a last name of Scofield.

The better known of the two is General John Schofield who died in Florida in 1906 and is buried in Arlington National Cemetery. He led Union troops in Missouri, Tennessee, Georgia and North Carolina during the Civil War. After the war, he served as U.S. Secretary of War under President Andrew Johnson.

Hiram Scofield died in Iowa in 1906 and is buried there. He served throughout the South during the war and commanded the 8th Louisiana Regiment Colored Troops while he was a colonel.

Thinking that General Scofield might have attained the rank of general after the Civil War, I looked through various databases. In searching through the National Park Service's database of Civil War veterans, you can find 444 men who served with the last name of Scofield. I checked Union pension records for Scofields in Maryland and Pennsylvania. Nine names came up Six had death dates listed that weren't in 1894. The other three had no death dates listed. Their names were Henry, Herman W. and Hunter J. However, no reference can be found that any of them were generals.

Marie Lancaster also spent much of her last years until her death in 2001 trying to figure out who General Scofield was.

"We never really could get to the bottom of anything," said her son, Robert.

He said his mother always felt a connection to the site because her grandfather was a Civil War veteran who was forgotten in a way.

When William Michael Loar returned home from fighting in the war for its entirety, he walked up a lane to a house and asked the two women there if he could have a bite to eat. The women were gracious and invited the war veteran in for supper.

As Loar sat down to eat at the kitchen table, he said to the older of the two women, "Mother, don't you know me?"

Neither Loar's wife or mother had recognized him after being gone for four years.

Loar was lucky. He was able to reunite with his family. The unknown veteran's family probably wondered what had happened to their brother/father/husband/son for the rest of their lives, never knowing he was buried beneath the ground and the wrong name on Meadow Mountain.

34

Maryland's Last Confederate Son

Some people tell stories of how their fathers fought in Vietnam, Korea, World War II or even World War I. Al Comer of Lavale, Maryland has them all beat.

"When I used to tell people my dad fought in the Civil War, they'd say, 'Aw, you're crazy!'" Al said.

Then he would start talking about birthdays and anniversaries and give the doubters a math lesson.

Al's father, James John Comer was born May, 2, 1847. He enlisted as an infantryman on June 1, 1861. He married Mary Ann Strole in 1869 and had eight children with her. After her death, James married Lucy Slye.

"She came to work for him to cook and take care of his family. She had a daughter younger than what she was," Al said.

Lucy and James had six children. Al was the youngest, born in 1921. At that time, James was 74 years old. While the Civil War is considered ancient history by many, for Al it is part of his childhood memories.

When Al was a youngster, his father was in the final years of his life and not traveling much. Al would stay home with his father while his mother went to church on Sundays.

"He'd teach me to play poker and tell me stories of the war," Al said.

James Comer joined the Confederate Army a month after his 14th birthday. He is listed as the youngest infantryman in Stonewall Jackson's 33rd Brigade, Company H, the "Page Grays." He was wounded in action at the Battle of Bull Run in July 1861 and then again at the Battle of Chancellorville in May 1863. He was taken prisoner in July

1864 near Harpers Ferry, West Virginia and then freed in a prisoner exchange in Elmira, New York in March 1865.

During the Civil War, James Comer guided raiding parties through the Shenandoah-Luray area. He would lead the Confederate soldiers to camps of Union soldiers where sometimes they would fight or just drive them off the Federal soldiers so the Confederates could take their rifles and gear.

One time, James and another soldier came across a dead Confederate soldier hanging on a fence.

"You hold my gun," the first soldier said.

He passed his rifle to James and began to pull the corpse off the fence. While James stood with the rifle, a Union sharpshooter shot the breech off the rifle.

Once while James was working on a burial detail, he and another soldier were carrying a coffin when a cannonball passed right through it.

Another time, a Union sergeant rode into his mother's yard with a patrol of eight men. They saw the horse and chickens his mother had and the sergeant ordered his men to gather them up. James Comer's mother pleaded with the soldiers to leave them.

James, who was in the kitchen in the house, stuck his rifle out the window and said, "I've got a rifle pointed at you, Sergeant. The first man who takes anything, I'll shoot you."

The sergeant looked at the rifle pointed at him and said, "Maybe we'd better not take them."

Then the patrol rode off and left the Comers alone.

While Al just always took it on his father's word that the stories were true, his great-niece Christa Wessel began researching her family's history. Then Christa's mother Nancy Lantz got involved. They came across muster rolls and handwritten journal pages from James. The rolls showed Al when his father was wounded and captured and the few pages of the journal gave him a first-hand look at the truth behind his father's stories.

"It didn't fully sink into me until I read these. That is what seals the deal for me," Al said.

One of the sections of the journal pages reads, "The Yankees charged us three times. We stood their charges and they broke and run. We captured about 5,000 prisoners, wagons and horses." The pages are undated so it is not known what battle James was writing about.

James Comer died in 1930. Lucy Comer died in 1977, still collecting a Confederate widow's pension of $50 a month.

Today, only 119 sons and daughters of Civil War soldiers are still alive and growing smaller each year, according to information from the Sons of Union Veterans of the Civil War and the Sons of Confederate Veterans organizations.

Al tried to follow in his father's footsteps and join the army during WWII, but a high school basketball injury had torn up his left knee and ankle and left him unfit for duty. Today, he is retired from the Kelly-Springfield Tire Company in Cumberland.

Al Comer is the only known child of a Civil War veteran, Union or Confederate, living in Maryland.

About the Author

James Rada, Jr. is the author of historical fiction and non-fiction history. They include the popular books *Saving Shallmar: Christmas Spirit in a Coal Town, Canawlers* and *Battlefield Angels: The Daughters of Charity Work as Civil War Nurses.*

He lives in Gettysburg, Pa., where he works as a freelance writer. Jim has received numerous awards from the Maryland-Delaware-DC Press Association, Associated Press, Maryland State Teachers Association and Community Newspapers Holdings, Inc. for his newspaper writing.

If you would like to be kept up to date on new books being published by James or ask him questions, he can be reached by e-mail at *jimrada@yahoo.com.*

To see James' other books or to order copies on-line, go to *www.jamesrada.com.*

If you liked ECHOES OF WAR DRUMS, you can find more stories at these FREE sites from James Rada, Jr.

JAMES RADA, JR.'S WEB SITE
www.jamesrada.com

The official web site for James Rada, Jr.'s books and news including a complete catalog of all his books (including eBooks) with ordering links. You'll also find free history articles, news and special offers.

TIME WILL TELL
historyarchive.wordpress.com

Read history articles by James Rada, Jr. plus other history news, pictures and trivia.

WHISPERS IN THE WIND
jimrada.wordpress.com

Discover more about the writing life and keep up to date on news about James Rada, Jr.

[1] *Cumberland Civilian and Telegraph*, April 25, 1861.
[2] *Ibid.* May 9, May 16, June 13, 1861.
[3] Harry Stegmaier, Jr., David Dean, Gordon Kershaw and John Wiseman, *Allegany County – A History* (Parsons, WV, 1976) 177.
[4] *Ibid.*, 181.
[5] *Valley News Echo*, June 1863.
[6] *Ibid.*
[7] Government Printing Office, *The War of the Rebellion: A Complilation of the Official Records of the Union and Confederate Armies, Series 1, Vol. 27, Pt. 2* (Washington, D.C., 1880-1901) 131.
[8] *Valley News Echo*, June 1863.
[9] James W. Thomas and T. J. C. Williams, *History of Allegany County* (Philadelphia, PA, 1923) 387.
[10] Government Printing Office, *The War of the Rebellion: A Complilation of the Official Records of the Union and Confederate Armies, Series 1, Vol. 27, Pt. 2* (Washington, D.C., 1880-1901) 183.
[11] William H. Lowdermilk, *A History of Cumberland, Maryland* (Baltimore, MD, 1878) 410.
[12] *Ibid.* pg. 411.
[13] *Ibid.* pg. 411.
[14] *Ibid.* pg. 411.
[15] *Ibid.* pg. 411.
[16] James W. Thomas and T. J. C. Williams, *History of Allegany County* (Philadelphia, PA, 1923) 388.
[17] *Valley News Echo*, June 1863.
[18] Harold L. Scott, Sr., *The Civil War Era in Cumberland, Maryland and nearby Keyser, West Virginia (1861-1865).* (Cumberland, Md. 2000) 159.
[19] Lowdermilk, 412.
[20] *Cumberland Union*, June 20, 27, July 4, 11, 1863.
[21] Lowdermilk, 412.
[22] Scott, 159.
[23] Simeon Miller Bright, "The McNeill Rangers: A Study in Confederate Guerilla Warfare," *http://www.wvculture.org/history/journal_wvh/wvh12-1.html* (2010). [Original Source: Simeon Miller Bright, "The McNeill Rangers: A Study in Confederate Guerilla Warfare," *West Virginia History*, Volume 12, Number 4 (July 1951), pp. 338-387.
[24] J. W. Duffey, *McNeill's Last Charge: An Account of a Daring Confederate in the Civil War* (Moorefield, 1944), p. 24-25.

[25] Robert N. Scott, *War of the Rebellion, Official Records of the Union and Confederate Armies*, Series I, Vol. 29 (Washington: Government Printing Office, 1886), p. 644.
[26] Hu Maxwell, Howard Llewellyn Swisher, *History of Hampshire County* (Morgantown: A.B. Boughner, 1897), p. 552.
[27] *Cumberland Sunday Times*, June 8, 1975.
[28] W. D. Vandiver, "Two Forgotten Heroes," *The Missouri Historical Review*, Volume 21, p. 409.
[29] *Moorefield Examiner*, August 23, 1895.
[30] *Ibid.*
[31] Vandiver, p. 411.
[32] *Valley Echo News,* February 1865.
[33] Vandiver, p. 413.
[34] Robert P. Broadwater, "To Catch a General – or Two," *America's Civil War*, May 2003, p. 48.
[35] Jesse C. McNeill, "Capture of Generals Kelley and Crook," *Confederate Veteran*, Volume XIV, 1906, 410.
[36] Roger U. Delauter, *McNeill's Rangers* (Lynchburg: H.E. Howard, 1986) p. 95.
[37] William Lowdermilk, A History of Cumberland, Maryland (Baltimore: Regional Publishing Company, 1971), p. 420.
[38] McNeill, p. 410.
[39] Duffey, pp. 9-10.
[40] Delauter, p. 97.
[41] Sylvester Myers, *Myers' History of West Virginia, Volume 1* (Wheeling: Wheeling News Lithograph Company, 1915), pg. 482.
[42] Maxwell and Swisher, pp. 676-677.
[43] *Ibid.*
[44] Lowdermilk, p. 421.
[45] Duffey, *p. 13.*
[46] Maxwell and Swisher, *pp.* 678-679.
[47] Duffey, p. 11.
[48] One of the men who arrested General Crook was Jacob Gassman, a former clerk in the Revere House and his uncle then owned the building. Sergeant Charles James Daily, who was also part of the group that arrested Crook, was the son of the hotel proprietor at that time and his sister, Mary, married Crook after the war.
[49] Delauter, p. 100.
[50] Maxwell and Swisher, pp. 680-681.
[51] Official Records, Series 1, Vol. 46 (Washington: Government Printing Office, 1886), p. 470.

[52] Maxwell and Swisher, pp. 680-681.
[53] *Valley News Echo*, February 1865.
[54] *Cumberland Sunday Times*, June 8, 1975.
[55] *Ibid.*
[56] Maxwell and Swisher, p. 682.
[57] *Cumberland Sunday Times,* June 8, 1975.
[58] Georgia's Blue and Gray Trail Presents America's Civil War: Brigadier General Benjamin Franklin Kelley, *http://blueandgraytrail.com/photo/4.*
[59] Delauter, p. 104.
[60] McNeill, p. 413.
[61] *Cumberland Evening Times*, June 4, 1925.
[62] William N. McDonald, *A History of the Laurel Brigade* (Baltimore: Self-published, 1907), 341.

www.ingramcontent.com/pod-product-compliance
Lightning Source LLC
Chambersburg PA
CBHW072335300426
44109CB00042B/1629